5 ∞

POWER IN COMMITTEES

AMERICAN POLITICS RESEARCH SERIES

POWER IN COMMITTEES

An Experiment
in the Governmental Process

JAMES DAVID BARBER

Yale University

Rand McNally & Company
Chicago, Illinois

AMERICAN POLITICS RESEARCH SERIES

Aaron Wildavsky, Series Editor

To
SARA NAISMITH BARBER AND JANE LEWIS BARBER
for questions and adventures

ACKNOWLEDGMENTS

FOR IDEAS AND inspiration, I am indebted to the many contributors to the burgeoning literature on small groups. Others have given me good advice more directly, but I am responsible for having taken or neglected it and, thus, for the whole content of this book. Fred I. Greenstein, Robert E. Lane, and Theodore Mills contributed many an uncompensated hour. Chris Argyris, Karl Bosworth, Theodore Lendler, and Oliver P. Williams were especially helpful in the design stage. Three experts on municipal government in Connecticut — William J. Reynolds, Beldon Schaffer, and John Walsh — each gave up a month of spring Saturdays to putting the design into effect. As research assistants in the experimental sessions, Larry Herrmann, P. J. Wooldridge, Jane Gillespie, Robert Packenham, Harry Blaney, William Liddle, and John Payne were wide awake, steady, and consistently cheerful. Ruth L. Davis, Arthur Goldberg, Joel Nelson, and Charles Raab did a careful job of compiling data. Hayward R. Alker was of great assistance in formulating statistical techniques, and Sarla Merchant, Carol Hopkins, and Judy Mallozzi of the Yale Computer Center were careful and patient with me and the machines. Comments on various early drafts by Richard A. Brody, William Flanigan, Bertram Gross, Harold Guetzkow, Charles F. Hermann, William H. Riker, and Aaron Wildavsky helped me shape the final analysis. Professors Brody, Greenstein, Lane, Wildavsky and Nelson W. Polsby gave me detailed comments on the final draft, for which I am most thankful. Lauren Kearney did an excellent job of typing the manuscript. Joan A. Bulger of Rand McNally edited the final copy, contributing clarity and grace to many a dim paragraph.

For financial support during this research I am grateful to the National Science Foundation, and particularly to Robert L. Hall for appreciating the vicissitudes of experimental research.

I am especially glad to thank the members of the twenty-four Connecticut boards of finance who participated in the field and laboratory sessions. Elsewhere[1] I have tried to pass on their practical advice, and I happily acknowledge their contributions to whatever is of scholarly value in this study.

This book is dedicated to half of my small group, with a large smile for their leader.

James David Barber

Washington, D.C.
July, 1965

[1]James D. Barber, "The Intellectual Work of the Board of Finance," *Connecticut Government*, XVI (1963), 1-4.

TABLE OF CONTENTS

List of Tables

POWER IN COMMITTEES

INTRODUCTION

IN MARCH 1965, President Johnson was reported to have been "waging war on the interagency committees for a good many months — without too much success." It was a losing battle: 163 federal interagency committees were abolished during the 1964 fiscal year, but 203 new ones came into existence, bringing the total to 560.[1] As of May 1961, despite previous reductions in the number of standing congressional committees, there were no fewer than 303 committee units of all types in Congress.[2] And among the 91,185 units of local government in the United States, as of 1962, there were more committees than anyone has cared to count.[3] Government by committees, it seems, is here to stay and likely to grow.

What happens when a group of public officials sit down around a table to decide something? Some years ago, I began looking for answers to this question by surveying previous work on committees. I found some studies of government committees, but few of them described the actual processes of decision-making in detail. On the other hand, there was a vast and complex literature, mainly in sociology and social psychology, on small groups other than government committees. Literally thousands of detailed, quantified studies existed, each with its tables and lists of hypotheses; exceptionally sophisticated techniques of observation and analysis had been developed. Could such techniques be applied to gather similar data, significant for political science, on the operations of committees in government? The present book is the result of one such effort. It is based on close observation of twelve local government committees as they worked on a set of standardized problems in a laboratory setting.

[1] Carroll Kilpatrick, "LBJ Asks Fewer Committees," *The Washington Post,* March 5, 1965, p. A4.
[2] "Congressional Reform," *Congressional Quarterly,* June 7, 1963, p. 10.
[3] See Roscoe C. Martin, "Intergovernmental Relations," in Stephen K. Bailey, ed., *American Politics and Government* (New York: Basic Books, 1965), p. 168.

In substance, the book is meant to play some part in answering the following questions:

What criteria do government committees actually make use of as they develop decisions? How can the work of a committee be organized so that maximum attention is directed to the main substantive choices?

How does a committee perceive and evaluate its power relations with other governmental bodies? What concepts guide the selection of strategies for enhancing a committee's relative power?

What part do highly abstract principles play in committee decision-making? Can one reasonably deduce probable power strategies from general beliefs about a community's power structure?

Within a government committee, what is the role of the chairman? What varieties of leadership do chairmen exhibit and how do their styles affect the process of decision-making?

What kinds of integration or cohesion are important for such groups? In particular, what part do affective ties and personal rewards play in building integration?

Can the many possible and plausible ways of defining and measuring the relative power of individual committee members be reduced to a few basic dimensions? What are the main resources and action patterns which support various forms of power?

Beyond the particular findings related to these questions, this book is an experiment in methodology, an attempt to illustrate in practical terms how a relatively new observational standpoint can be used to generate data useful for a wide variety of political science purposes.

The phenomenal growth of tested generalizations about political behavior owes much to the development of new research methods. The pioneering work of V. O. Key, Jr., in analyzing relationships between voting and demographic variables,[4] has produced a rich store of findings and stimulated historians to look again, in a different way, at their explanations for past election outcomes.[5] The sample survey has revealed the relatively stable substructure of public attitudes over which the forces of political change ebb and flow.[6] Group interviews of members of various population categories show how the same stimulus can produce markedly different responses from farmers and housewives,

[4]V. O. Key, Jr., *Southern Politics in State and Nation* (New York: Knopf, 1949).

[5]Lee Benson, "Research Problems in American Political Historiography," in Mirra Komarovsky, ed., *Common Frontiers in the Social Sciences* (Glencoe, Ill.: Free Press, 1957).

[6]Angus Campbell, Philip E. Converse, Warren E. Miller, and Donald E. Stokes, *The American Voter* (New York: Wiley, 1960).

businessmen and students.[7] Computer simulation of opinion-formation processes opens up a new set of possibilities for understanding the dynamic aspects of political campaigning.[8] In the study of local communities it is now feasible to collect a wide range of illuminating data, by asking leaders to rate one another,[9] by analyzing the history of particular decisions,[10] and by a variety of anthropological techniques.[11] Observers fortunately placed, as active participants[12] or privileged companions of key leaders,[13] have brought forth a picture of government action far removed from that of the older civics texts. Quantitative analyses — of roll call votes,[14] of judicial decisions,[15] of budgeting,[16] of changing frequencies of symbols appearing in the press,[17] of the movement of materials and messages across political boundaries[18] — all have stimulated new and significant insights into the workings of political institutions. Qualitative studies based on psychoanalytic and biographical data,[19] extended depth interviews with citizens carefully selected to represent common attitudes,[20] briefer but flexible interviews with legislators[21] and administrators,[22] and discussions with groups of decision-makers[23] have contributed important facts concerning the meanings men attach to their political actions. The list is

[7]Friedrich Pollock, *Gruppenexperiment* (Frankfurt: Europaische Verlagsanstalt, 1955).

[8]Ithiel de Sola Pool, Robert P. Abelson, and Samuel L. Popkin, *Candidates, Issues and Strategies* (Cambridge: M.I.T. Press, 1964).

[9]Robert Presthus, *Men at the Top* (New York: Oxford University Press, 1964).

[10]Robert A. Dahl, *Who Governs?* (New Haven, Conn.: Yale University Press, 1961).

[11]Arthur J. Vidich and Joseph Bensman, *Small Town in Mass Society* (Princeton, N.J.: Princeton University Press, 1958).

[12]Harold Stein, ed., *Public Administration and Policy Development* (New York: Harcourt, Brace, 1952).

[13]Raymond E. Wolfinger, *The Politics of Progress* (New Haven, Conn.: Yale University Press, forthcoming).

[14]David B. Truman, *The Congressional Party* (New York: Wiley, 1959).

[15]Glendon A. Schubert, ed., *Judicial Decision-Making* (New York: Free Press of Glencoe, 1963).

[16]Aaron Wildavsky, *The Politics of the Budgetary Process* (Boston: Little, Brown, 1964).

[17]Richard L. Merritt, *Symbols of American Community, 1735-1775* (forthcoming).

[18]Bruce M. Russett, *Community and Contention* (Cambridge: M.I.T. Press, 1963).

[19]Alexander L. George and Juliette L. George, *Woodrow Wilson and Colonel House* (New York: John Day, 1956).

[20]Robert E. Lane, *Political Ideology* (New York: Free Press of Glencoe, 1962).

[21]Donald R. Matthews, *U.S. Senators and Their World* (Chapel Hill: University of North Carolina Press, 1960).

[22]W. Lloyd Warner, Paul P. Van Riper, Norman H. Martin, and Orvis F. Collins, *The American Federal Executive* (New Haven, Conn.: Yale University Press, 1963).

[23]Charles L. Clapp, *The Congressman* (Washington: Brookings Institution, 1963).

continually growing as researchers invent and apply new approaches in a variety of contexts. The result is an unabashed methodological eclecticism among political scientists who are ready to try whatever techniques, wherever they may originate, that promise to add significantly to our knowledge of how men govern themselves.

In recent years small groups approaches to the study of political phenomena have developed rapidly, along three main lines. Some scholars have concentrated on the existent body of small groups literature, largely derived from experimental work with subjects other than political decision-makers, to see what insights, hypotheses, questions, and answers they might suggest for political scientists. For example, Ralph K. White and Ronald Lippitt, in their reanalysis of data from experiments with clubs of eleven-year-old boys, interject sections of "political commentary," applying their evidence speculatively to such questions as "Can the danger of dictatorship be combated more realistically by adding to, or subtracting from, the strength of the more or less democratic governments in the non-Communist world?"[24] Secondly, some researchers — particularly Harold Guetzkow and his associates — have managed to observe directly actual government officials in a variety of controlled decision-making and role-playing experiments, and, thus, can draw more immediately compelling conclusions about actual decision processes.[25] Finally, some political scientists who do not use experimental techniques nevertheless find certain concepts and propositions derived from small groups studies useful in analyzing their data. The current work of Richard Fenno and his associates on integration in congressional committees is a good example.[26]

Each of these approaches appears promising. In the first chapter of this book, I express considerable doubt about a fourth possibility: the direct transfer of findings from experimental, *ad hoc* small groups studies to government committees. While political scientists have generally been overly skeptical about small groups methods, I think they are right in moving cautiously from laboratory findings to conclusions about action in the field.

The data for this book are drawn from meetings of twelve different Connecticut boards of finance (local government budget-making com-

[24]Ralph K. White and Ronald Lippitt, *Autocracy and Democracy* (New York: Harper, 1960), p. 137.

[25]Harold Guetzkow, C. F. Alger, R. A. Brody, R. C. Noel, and R. C. Snyder, *Simulation in International Relations* (Englewood Cliffs, N.J.: Prentice-Hall, 1963).

[26]Richard F. Fenno, Jr., "The House Appropriations Committee as a Political System: The Problem of Integration," *American Political Science Review*, LVI (1962), 310-24.

mittees) held in the Yale Interaction Laboratory in the spring of 1962. A detailed description of the data and methodology is presented in Chapter I and complete questionnaires appear in Appendix C.

The theme or organizing concept of the remaining chapters is political power, a topic of some interest and much frustrating complexity for political scientists. These chapters move from the relatively obvious to the relatively obscure forms of power, beginning, in the second chapter, with the down-to-earth process of making a budget. In this chapter, the problem for each group is a familiar one: to allocate limited resources among competing demands. The findings concern the criteria actually expressed and employed in arriving at agreed-upon budget figures. In Chapters III and IV, we consider a broader set of criteria, namely the values and perceptions which committee members bring to bear when they try to define their power relationships with other agencies of government. Thus, the analysis moves from the concrete and the specific — who gets how much money for what — to the problem of determining just where the committee stands in the power structure of the local government. The focus is on the operative distribution of power — the practical relations of conflict and compromise — as seen through the eyes of the participants.

Up to this point the book is about topics at the forefront of the members' attention and interest. In Chapters V, VI, and VII, we turn to matters which they rarely considered in any systematic way, that is, the distribution and exercise of power within the committee itself. The clearest focus of interpersonal power here is the chairman. Within the committee, his is the only formally differentiated position, so that we might expect him to exercise considerable influence over his fellow members. In fact, as the evidence shows, there is a marked difference in the performance and the impact of chairmen who make the most of their roles and chairmen who confine themselves to routine presiding. In Chapter VI, the analysis progresses to relationships among all the members. In what sense is a committee unified or integrated? What are the main determinants of the kind of unity which enables a committee to operate effectively? What do members get out of their participation that motivates them to work well with their colleagues?

The most complex and difficult (but perhaps the most interesting) power analysis is reserved for Chapter VII, Dimensions of Interpersonal Power. Here the focus is on power relationships between each individual member of a committee and all the other members. The topic is complex because there are so many possible ways of conceptualizing and measuring the various aspects of political power. In this chapter, measurements for a fairly large collection (45) of power variables are related to one another empirically, so that we can see which of them highlight significant distinctions in power, and how much overlap there is among theoretically different measures. Out of this evidence emerge five basic power dimensions, each empirically and theoretically distinct. Now we are able to consider (*a*) the types of actions initiated by a member which tend to enhance his power in each of the five dimensions, and (*b*) the resources and personal characteristics associated with each variety of power.

Readers interested in various controversies in contemporary political science may find the following chapters of special interest: on incrementalism and rationality, Chapter II; on community power structure, Chapters III and IV; on directive versus non-directive leadership, Chapter V; on participation, task specialization, and group cohesion, Chapter VI; on the definition of power, Chapter VII.

Methodologically, the chapters move from the simple to the complex. Chapter II on budgetary criteria and Chapter III on the cultural aspects of power could have been written from field transcriptions, without ever bringing the groups into the laboratory, provided topics and time periods were under careful control. The method used here is a simple form of content analysis, with illustrations of dominant themes. The need for the laboratory setting, i.e., the opportunity for close scoring of interaction, becomes evident in Chapter IV. Throughout the book, the statistical methods are elementary, except for the factor analysis in Chapter VII, which is easy to understand once one grasps a few basic ideas.

The reader who wishes to explore the small groups literature further might begin with two works by political scientists, Sidney Verba's *Small Groups and Political Behavior*[27] and Robert Golembiewski's *The Small Group*[28]; both books were of much assistance in planning the research reported here. Two clear and interesting analyses of social psychological aspects are *A Social Psychology of Group Processes for Decision-Making*[29] by Barry E. Collins and Harold Guetzkow, and *The Social Psychology of Groups*[30] by John W. Thibaut and Harold H. Kelley. Of the several collections of small groups readings, I have found the following most useful: A. Paul Hare, *Handbook of Small Group Research*[31]; Hare, Edgar F. Borgatta, and

[27](Princeton, N.J.: Princeton University Press, 1961).
[28](Chicago: University of Chicago Press, 1962).
[29](New York: Wiley, 1964).
[30](New York: Wiley, 1961).
[31](New York: Free Press of Glencoe, 1962).

Robert F. Bales, eds., *Small Groups*[32]; and Dorwin Cartwright and Alvin Zander, eds., *Group Dynamics: Research and Theory.*[33] For a recent review of political science applications, see Richard C. Snyder, "Experimental Techniques and Political Analysis," in the issue of the *Annals of the American Academy of Political and Social Science* titled *The Limits of Behavioralism in Political Science.*[34] On budgeting calculations and strategies, Aaron Wildavsky's *The Politics of the Budgetary Process* is by far the best source; from it I have borrowed more ideas than the footnotes indicate.

[32](New York: Knopf, 1955).
[33](Evanston, Ill.: Row, Peterson, 1953).
[34](Philadelphia: American Academy of Political and Social Science, 1962).

CHAPTER I

Government Committees in the Small Groups Laboratory

How MIGHT SMALL groups research be useful to the political scientist who is trying to understand the behavior of government committees?

In government, committees abound and proliferate. In contemporary social science, laboratory studies of small decision-making groups abound even more plentifully and proliferate at an even more alarming rate. We know that government committees play roles of central concern to the political scientist. And we recognize that the small groups "movement" has attracted some eminently qualified scholars. Yet many — probably most — political scientists remain skeptical about the applicability of small groups techniques and findings to the problems of their discipline. I would argue that, although the direct transfer of *findings* from the typical laboratory experiment to politics is unwarranted, there are ways to utilize some small groups *techniques* to generate politically interesting findings.

Hypotheses generated in the typical small groups laboratory study are unlikely to be confirmed by observers of the typical government committee (I shall soon make appropriate qualifications), because there are so many highly relevant differences between the subjects and their activities in the two arenas. Compare any government committee with the typical small groups laboratory study, in which —

    1. The *subjects* are college students. Thus they are younger and, perhaps even more significantly, all about the same age. They are very close to one another in social status and educational level. They have not yet developed strong personal identities.

They lack experience in making group decisions with important consequences to themselves or to anyone else. They move into the laboratory from an environment in which experimental research is respected, discussion about hypothetical problems is continual, and the expression and examination of tentative ideas is encouraged. They are used to being ordered about, told what to read and discuss, where to go, when to stop and start. They do not expect to understand fully why they are asked to do these particular things. In many cases, they have recently been studying psychology or sociology quite intensively, so that – hopefully – they are rather sensitive to certain personal and interpersonal events.

2. These subjects are brought together for the first time by a professor – often their own professor. Their only formal *responsibility* is to him. All of them become members of the group at the same moment. As strangers they have no group traditions, have established no group structure, and have no basis (other than what they can see) for predicting how the other subjects will respond. They anticipate that the group will disband after one or a few meetings. In some cases they have been required to attend, in others they are offered a monetary reward, and in others yet they simply volunteer for an interesting experience advertised by a brief and vague description.

3. The *instructions* are for the group to discuss and solve a problem which is sprung on them shortly after they assemble. The task may be a puzzle, a human relations problem, some sort of arithmetical or verbal manipulation. Trivial or not, it is in any case not an outgrowth of the group's past deliberations (since it has none), it has no implications for the future, and (most often) it has no anticipated impact on anyone outside the group other than the experimenter. The task rarely relates in any direct way to the skills, interests, or knowledge the group members possess. Thus, it is not especially salient for or congruent with this *kind* of group (i.e., collegians), much less adapted to the practices or characteristics of any particular group. Typically the task is self-contained, that is, the participants are expected to use only such information as is presented with the problem.

4. The researcher instructs the group to reach a descision within a specified *time*. The task, then, is designed to be solvable in thirty minutes or an hour. No rules of procedure or group organization are imposed. No chairman is appointed or elected,

no division of labor suggested. The expectation appears to be that all members will interact as equals.

5. While they are talking, the subjects are being *observed* by the researcher they know and others they do not know, for purposes they understand only vaguely. The observers are hidden in a strange position—behind a one-way mirror. The subject cannot see how the observers are reacting to him, and in any case he does not know what they are looking for. He is assured that he will not be held responsible for his remarks, that they will not even be attributed to him. Nevertheless, he anticipates that what he says will be scrutinized repeatedly, and in great detail—else why is it being recorded?—by persons he does not know.

It is easier to specify these characteristics—all of which contrast markedly with the typical government committee meeting—than it is to estimate what effects they have on the process and products of group decision-making. Will the members of a laboratory group be more relaxed and playful because they know they have no commitment to the group or its tasks, or more restrained and tense because they are being closely observed and evaluated? Does their passive relationship with the observing researcher lead them to strive to produce a better solution because they want to please him or to hold back their efforts because they resent his domination? The evidence on such matters is contradictory.[1] I am not persuaded by the "feeling" on the part of experimenters that subjects soon get used to the laboratory and proceed as if they were not being observed. I have felt the same thing in watching local government committees in the laboratory, but distrust the emotion as too self-serving to be entirely credible.

What we have in the typical small groups laboratory experiment, then, is a temporary collection of late-adolescent strangers given a puzzle to solve under bizarre conditions in a limited time during their first meeting while being peered at from behind a mirror. In many experiments the situation is even more elaborately contrived, so that we wonder whether the results would apply to any population beyond the laboratory. How likely is it that the persons who conform most readily to majority influences in estimating the movement of a point of light in a dark room are also those who conform to majority political opinions in their neighborhoods?[2] And it is more than merely plausible

[1] See the summary of findings on the effects of an audience in Gardner Lindzey, ed., *Handbook of Social Psychology* (Reading, Mass.: Addison-Wesley, 1954), II, 750.

[2] A brief bibliography on the auto-kinetic effect appears in A. Paul Hare, *Handbook of Small Group Research* (New York: Free Press of Glencoe, 1962), p. 26.

that the kinds of subjects selected and the conditions under which they work have profound effects on the generalizability of findings—on leadership, participation rates, satisfaction, effectiveness, and so on. For example:

1. Numerous studies of initially leaderless small groups show a marked differentiation between a "task leader" who contributes ideas and guidance but is not well-liked, and a "social-emotional leader" who has the opposite characteristics. But in seventy-two real committees in business and government the chairman ordinarily performed both roles, and members were dissatisfied when he failed to do so.[3]

2. In three-person laboratory discussion groups, a tendency toward the development of a stable coalition between the two high participants, and the exclusion of the third member has been found. But in real three-person family groups (parents and son), no such stable pattern developed.[4]

3. In a study of children's clubs, satisfaction and work performance were strongly affected by leadership styles (autocratic, democratic, and laissez-faire). But adults assembled as juries to hear and decide a simulated case were unaffected by variations in the same leadership styles.[5]

4. Effective and ineffective aircraft crews, so classified on the basis of their combat experience, actual success in missions, and ratings of superiors, did not differ in their "problem-solving scores" in a laboratory experiment.[6]

For all these reasons, we should be most cautious in transferring findings directly from the small, artificial laboratory group to the government committee. As sources of insights, ideas, and hypotheses to be tested in real committees, the laboratory studies can be valuable. But a naive lifting of results from the one realm to the other is premature.

[3]See Philip E. Slater, "Role Differentiation in Small Groups," in A. Paul Hare, Edgar F. Borgatta, and Robert F. Bales, eds., *Small Groups* (New York: Knopf, 1955); and Leonard Berkowitz, "Sharing Leadership in Small Decision-Making Groups," *Journal of Abnormal and Social Psychology*, XLVIII (1953), 231-38.

[4]See Theodore M. Mills, "Power Relations in Three-Person Groups," *American Sociological Review*, XIX (1954), 657-67; and F. L. Strodtbeck, "The Family as a Three-Person Group," *American Sociological Review*, XIX (1954), 23-29.

[5]See Ralph K. White and Ronald Lippitt, *Autocracy and Democracy* (New York: Harper, 1960), pt. II; and William Bevan *et al.*, "Jury Behavior as a Function of the Prestige of the Foreman and the Nature of His Leadership," *Journal of Public Law*, VII (1958), 419-49.

[6]See E. P. Torrance, "Perception of Group Functioning as a Predictor of Group Performance," *Journal of Social Psychology*, XLII (1955), 271-82.

It would be easy at this point to dismiss the whole collection of small groups studies as irrelevant for political science, but that would also be premature, for two reasons. In the first place, better research techniques for understanding how committees work are desperately needed. Much progress has been made in the close analysis of the *decision products* of government committees (by the statistical examination of roll call votes, Supreme Court decisions, and so on[7]), but less is known in a highly systematic, verifiable way about the *process* which intervenes between the initiation and the resolution of a committee decision. For information on the latter we must usually rely on historical-institutional accounts or on incomparable observations of this or that committee. We need techniques which will catch more of the actual interaction which goes into making a committee decision, and we need to produce findings which can be independently verified by other observers, will apply to more than one committee, and can be expressed quantitatively. If the typical small groups study is too contrived and artificial, the typical political science study of the process of decision-making has perhaps been too loose and general.

A second reason for looking again at the small groups approaches is that many of them diverge markedly from the "typical" situation which has been described. In many studies the subjects are "real" people[8] and sometimes "real" groups.[9] The tasks they are assigned are not all trivial games.[10] Small groups have been observed covertly[11] or with minimum disturbance in the natural setting.[12] Furthermore, there are many different types of government committees. The jury, for example, may be fairly close in certain respects to the *ad hoc* experimental group, while the analogy from the latter to the Supreme Court is much more tenuous. As these gaps are narrowed, the bridging infer-

[7]Cf., for example, Eloise Snyder, "The Supreme Court as a Small Group," *Social Forces,* XXXVI (1958), 232-38.

[8]E.g., the railroad foremen studied by E. F. Harris and E. A. Fleishman, "Human Relations Training and the Stability of Leadership Patterns," *Journal of Applied Psychology,* XXXIX (1955), 20-25.

[9]E.g., B-29 bomber crews, in Dorothy M. Kipnis, "Interaction between Members of Bomber Crews as a Determinant of Sociometric Choice," *Human Relations,* X (1957), 263-70.

[10]E.g., psychotherapy, in J. L. Singer and G. D. Goldman, "Experimentally Contrasted Social Atmospheres in Group Psychotherapy with Chronic Schizophrenics," *Journal of Social Psychology,* XL (1954), 23-37.

[11]E.g., by "camp counselors," in M. Sherif, "Experiments in Group Conflict," *Scientific American,* CXCV (1956), 54-58.

[12]E.g., husbands and wives discussing politics in the home, in James G. March, "Husband-Wife Interaction over Political Issues," *Public Opinion Quarterly,* XVII (1953), 461-70.

ences become more plausible. But we are still left with many uncertainties as we move from the aircraft crew to the small party caucus, from the family to the legislative committee, from the solution of human relations problems in the laboratory to real administrative decisions in a bureaucracy.

Rather than lifting findings from small groups research, political scientists might consider imitating some of the methods of small groups research. For example:

1. *Subjects* who are already operating as government committees, or who are likely to be, or who resemble closely those who are, might be recruited for observation.

2. The *tasks* for such groups might be ones they are in fact responsible for making, or tasks similar to those they make, or tasks drawing in some way on their past experience and future expectations.

3. The *observation procedures* might be arranged to minimize manipulation and the impact of the setting and observers, to simulate as nearly as possible the normal procedures for committee decision-making, and/or to discover if possible what effects the research procedures actually have on the subjects.

Arranging such research requires a series of difficult decisions as one strives to maximize both comparability and realism at the same time. In the following paragraphs, some of the pitfalls and possibilities are illustrated by the description of the research design for this study of local government committees. The subjects here were the members of a dozen Connecticut boards of finance—real officials in their real groups. The tasks dealt directly with their regular functions. And their procedures were their own, performed while being closely but unobtrusively observed.

RECRUITING SUBJECTS

Perhaps one of the biggest breakthroughs in recent political science has been in gaining access to public officials. Increasingly, political scientists have found that it *is* possible to get at the President, congressmen, senators, mayors, state legislators, local politicians, national convention delegates, and other officials, and to gather systematic data from or about them. Persistence and planning have paid off in a wealth of new data. In this particular study the problem was to persuade twelve complete local government committees to hold meetings in the small groups laboratory. To recruit subjects at other levels of government, or for less intensive observation, other techniques would be appropriate, although perhaps some of the following procedures would apply.

Connecticut had, in early 1962, 131 towns with boards of finance consisting of five to eleven elected members responsible for town budgeting and financial policy. Since I had served on my own town's board and had visited eleven other boards to make field recordings, I had some idea of the difficulty in getting a board into the small groups laboratory. The members would not come for a personal fee. They would not come, I judged, for the sole purpose of advancing knowledge, although they would want to feel they were making some contribution. Perhaps they would not come in any case, most of them being busy businessmen with other uses for their Saturdays.

Three appeals seemed most likely to be effective. First, the boards might be interested in improving their own operations or solving their own particular problems. Thus, a flyer described the projected series of meetings as "Conferences on Board of Finance Operations and Responsibilities." The program included an informal meeting with an expert consultant on town finance (the three consultants were described in detail), and an "evaluation session" for developing suggestions for improvement, as well as two "problem-solving sessions" (the main simulation). Each participant was promised a report on the completed project. Second, I felt that while the members would be put off by a direct offer of money to each individually, they would like to take something concrete back to their towns and would accept travel expenses. An "award" of $100 to be "contributed to any worthy cause chosen by the board" was offered to those boards attending with no more than one absentee. This offer also indicated to them the seriousness of the project. Third, the chance to visit a university campus and have a look around appeared appealing. Thus the meeting with the consultant was to take place at luncheon in one of the residential college dining halls.

Anticipating objections, the program description gave answers to the following questions: What are the purposes of this program of conferences? How might this program contribute to knowledge about local government in the United States? Who is conducting and supporting this program? Has this type of program been done before? From what kinds of communities will the participating boards be selected? How will the problem-solving sessions be conducted? Why is $100 offered for boards which participate with no more than one member absent? What will be done with the results of this research? What practical help might this program provide for boards of finance? The answers were straightforward—for example, that the problem-solving and evaluation sessions would be observed and recorded— stressing about equally the research and the practical pay-offs.

A package containing a cover letter, a copy of the program description for each member, a mailback form for indicating interest, date preference and the probability that all members could attend, and a stamped return envelope was sent to each of the 131 board chairmen. Fifty-two replied that their members were interested and could attend, with varying degrees of probability. Six said they could not come. The generous response allowed me to select only boards which indicated that all members could definitely attend at a schedulable date. Thirteen boards were picked: one as a pretest, and four from each of three population categories. Excluding the pretest group, only seven of the ninety-two participants invited were subsequently absent, no more than two from any one board. Following up the initial inquiry with telephone calls, letters to all members, reminders, maps of the campus, and so on, all helped to insure attendance.

The difficulties in generalizing results from such a selective set of committees are evident. It is unlikely that we shall soon be able to sample randomly from the universe of committees on any level. The boards which answered my inquiry most enthusiastically were, I suspect, atypical in the direction of greater interest in their work, more intense identification with their communities, a more positive attitude toward the university and its symbols, as well as greater availability (proximity, free time, and so on). It may be that these differences should be taken into account in the interpretation of data at certain points. In deciding what appeals to stress, one shapes the response. At this stage it is probably wise to use those honest appeals which will maximize the pool of available committees, despite the warping this introduces.[13]

Perhaps more important are the problems of defining the boundaries of the committee and making strong efforts to get every member to attend. The first problem, which Robert Golembiewski has discussed at length,[14] is especially significant for government committees: the *formal* membership may exclude persons such as clerks, secretaries, *ex officio* members, and so on, who are however normally present in the group. The committee may lapse into confusion in their absence. My decision was to invite anyone who regularly attended the meetings in some official capacity (thus, however, excluding the press) in order to

[13]An alternative approach would be to select a random sample of committees, and then make intensive efforts to get them to participate. The risk of absenteeism might be great, however.

[14]*The Small Group* (Chicago: University of Chicago Press, 1962), pp. 34-68.

re-create as nearly as possible the natural group. This introduces certain ambiguities of role, function, and status, but exclusion of these quasi-members would distort the operations of a group used to their presence. Interpretation is harder, but the data are more realistic. The problem of absentees can be severe: only two of one committee's six members showed up for the pretest session. Apparently they considered themselves delegates to a conference. Fortunately, this was not a severe problem with the other boards, perhaps because of the conditions established for the $100 award. This or some similar method for insuring the presence of the full committee seems essential—unless one wishes to study only active minorities.

TASKS

In designing tasks for committee simulation we are caught between our desire for comparability and our desire for realism. Comparability demands that each committee perform the same tasks. Realism demands that each committee be observed doing actual committee work, that is, making real, binding decisions as it usually does. Obviously these demands are at odds, and some compromise is necessary.

Boards of finance perform a wide variety of tasks, ranging from setting the tax rate to choosing a cover design for the Town Report. Field observations had shown that they spend a good deal of time gathering information (such as hearing testimony by the chief executive, budget requests from town agencies, expert advice on building programs) rather than making decisions. To ask each board to hold an actual business meeting in the laboratory would result in a confusing variety of discussions on different topics. Nor could their calendars be rearranged to schedule a real decision-making session for my convenience. My problem, then, was to invent tasks which (1) involved decision-making, (2) were comparable from group to group, and (3) were similar in certain ways to regular board of finance tasks.

Points (1) and (2) required that each problem-solving session end with a group decision and that the tasks and time periods be the same for all groups. Point (3) was more difficult. Obviously the tasks should have group-relevant content, draw upon past experience, and involve implications for the future. But I could not in fact require the boards to come to binding decisions and they were sure to perceive this. To compensate somewhat for this artificiality, the tasks would have to be especially interesting to them, salient enough to bring out their conflicting viewpoints and patterns of interpersonal relations. Furthermore, I wanted several different tasks, in order to see what if any changes in group structure and process took place as the board moved from one type of problem to another. I decided finally on three tasks — a "normal" task, a "hot issue," and a session of group introspection — each to last for thirty minutes.

Task 1: The "Normal" Task

The problem here is to discover what types of significant decisions all the committees perform as a regular part of their work, and to pose a standard problem which will stimulate them to make similar decisions in the laboratory. In the case of the boards of finance, the first of these problems was easy to solve: the main regular task for all these boards is budget-making. Each board reviews requests from town government agencies and recommends reductions (normally they are not permitted to recommend raises) to the town's legislative body.

Stimulating realistic activity on an obviously hypothetical problem was more difficult. Knowing that they would not in fact be held responsible for their laboratory decisions, the members of a board might quickly come to an easy decision. For instance, if asked to review an imaginary request for funds, they might simply approve the request without controversy, whereas their normal tendency would be to scrutinize every request carefully, looking for savings. I decided on a strategy of *exaggerating the committee's normal tendency*. Normally they look for moderate savings; I asked them to look for sizable ones. Normally they work to reduce budgets; I asked them to reduce them severely. In this case, then, an element of artificiality is introduced to compensate for another, inevitable artificiality. The alternative, it seems to me, is to pretend that the latter does not exist.

A copy of the board's own most recent set of town budget recommendations was distributed to each of the participants. They were instructed to suppose it necessary to reduce their recommendations by $1000 and to decide exactly where this cut should be made. After completing this, they were asked to continue reducing the budget drastically, down to "those funds absolutely indispensable for the most basic town services." Most boards fell rapidly to work on this problem, examining the figures, proposing cuts, discussing and deciding.

The key feature here is that the members of the committee perform an operation on familiar materials (in this case, their own budget) with a familiar purpose (here, to find savings). The purpose is exaggerated to stimulate interest and intragroup controversy. And the deliberations involve at least some future commitment: Member X's suggestion that the public works department could really get along without so much money would be remembered by his colleagues at an appropriate future time. Thus the task is formally the same for all groups, but, at the same time, it is based on the previous experience of each, is decided in the context of their own store of information, and has significant implications for their future.

Task 2: The "Hot Issue"

We want to observe not only the "normal" operations of a committee, but also their deliberations on especially controversial matters. Typically these are discussed only in executive session, and, to strangers from another community, the committee will tend to present a front of solidarity. Special techniques are necessary, therefore, to stimulate frank discussion of "hot issues" in the laboratory.

The controversy which the committees dealt with in this research concerned public education costs. By far the largest single item in the town budget is the expense for public education, despite the fact that much aid comes from the state and federal governments. Under Connecticut law, with minor exceptions, town educational appropriations have a special status. The board of finance may examine the board of education's budget in detail and suggest specific reductions, but they may *enforce* a reduction only in the total school appropriation. The school board is thereafter free to transfer funds from category to category, despite the finance board's recommendations. This situation has led to considerable strife. At the time of our laboratory sessions, the matter was in the state courts and there was talk of legislative action. Thus, relations between the two boards was a current hot issue, a matter of considerable concern to the members, and they might be expected to express themselves readily about it.

But here again it seemed important to take the exact laboratory situation into account. The members of the board would be performing as representatives of their community before an audience of strangers. In this encounter, expressions of their frank (operative) views about their home-town school board might be inhibited. I decided, therefore, to use a projective technique: members were to suppose that their advice was being sought by a community in another state regarding the best practicable relationship between the two boards. Three proposals had been advanced, one approximating the actual Connecticut system, one freeing the school board of any financial ties with the town government, and a third placing educational expenses in the same category as those of any other town government department. As their recommendation the subjects might adopt one of these proposals, amend them, or invent an entirely new one.[15] This task elicited, in most cases, the most spirited discussion of the day. The three boards with the most harmonious working relations with their school boards (as judged from newspaper accounts and board minutes by an independent researcher who knew nothing of their laboratory discussion) adopted approximately their present system for the mythical town, while the four boards with histories of interboard conflict adopted solutions severely restricting the school board's freedom to make transfers.

The difficulties in getting real government committees to handle hot issues in the laboratory may be overcome to some extent by such a device. The hypothetical nature of the problem is here both a problem and an advantage: it is introduced as one artificiality in order to counteract another artificiality—the presence of observers—in the laboratory situation. This may be compounding errors. But the alternative would seem to be pretending that the observers do not exist.

Task 3: Group Introspection

Observation of groups performing simulated tasks is one technique for gathering data on their decision-making; another is to ask them directly how they go about making their decisions. The group interview may reveal factors missed in the discussion. For example, the group may show a good deal of disagreement and antagonism in dealing with simulated tasks. It would be helpful to know how the members themselves perceive and evaluate such expressions. The group interview may provide data indicating, for instance, that members place a high value on being "independent-minded," "outspoken," "willing to stand up and be counted," or, on the other hand, the group may value "harmony," "reasonableness," "not getting into personalities," "non-partisanship," and so on. To get at such dimensions of perception and evaluation, the group interview can be useful. It is, however, a task rather different from the other two types, posing special problems of design.

After the first two tasks were completed, the board of finance members filled out long questionnaires,[16] went to lunch with the consultant, and returned to the laboratory for an evaluation session

[15]For the text of this problem, which was given to each member, see Appendix B. I also read this text aloud to each group.
[16]For the complete text of the questionnaires, see Appendix C.

which I led non-directively. To begin the discussion I gave each person a list of questions[17] referring to "factors which have been found to contribute to effective group decision-making," such as "getting a clear picture of the problem to be solved," "consideration of available time," "acceptance of suggestions and criticism," "relations of chairman and members." I then asked them whether they had experienced any such problems, or had any suggestions in this regard.

Their initial reactions were interesting. Typically, someone began with a joke. Then, after some hesitation, a senior member would begin to expound on problems the board *once* had (but not now), or problems some *other* committee was experiencing, or problems the board definitely did *not* have to worry about. I allowed this to proceed for awhile, before challenging the general implication that the members of the board were entirely satisfied by asking whether there was not one item on the list in regard to which the board was less than 100 per cent perfect. This ploy brought first denials that they were paragons, and then a slow, hesitant unwinding of inhibitions as they explored their difficulties. All in all, it was a stressful period — resulting, however, in the identification and mutual examination of some recurrent but rarely examined problems.

The task here was very close to home, too close for comfort. The members found it much easier to practice their decision-making techniques in the first two tasks than to discuss them in the third. Thus the discussion provided a good opportunity to observe the group under pressure, eventually brought out some central dimensions of committee culture, and made possible the observation of the effects of the presence of an inquiring stranger on the chairman and other members. Despite its differences from the other two tasks, it shares certain characteristics with them: the problems are of immediate significance to the group, call upon their past experience, and refer in a direct way to their future performance.

OBSERVATION PROCEDURES

The object here is to accomplish the purposes of the research with a minimum of disturbance of the normal group procedures. Some of the disturbances introduced — the time limit, the imposed tasks, the requirement of a group decision — have been mentioned. These would seem to be the minimum interferences necessary for generating com-

---

[17]This list was adapted from E. P. Torrance, "Methods of Conducting Critiques of Group Problem-Solving Performance," *Journal of Applied Psychology*, XXVII (1953), 394-98.

parable findings for several groups. Using these methods, committees could be observed and tape recorded in the field, in their natural settings.

The laboratory setting, particularly the use of one-way mirrors, has several advantages, however. The boards of finance research used the Bales Interaction Process Analysis system of observation,[18] in which two scorers record on a moving tape each unit of interaction in one of twelve standard categories,[19] noting the initiator and the recipient of the remark. The scorers must look directly at the group members, concentrating intensely on their verbal and physical acts, while making rapid notations. The result is a collection of detailed, sequential, attributed, quantitative, and classified data which can be analyzed from a variety of viewpoints.

In addition, an observer is needed to match tape-recorded comments to the persons speaking them. The typed transcript of a meeting of a group of, say, nine members is useless unless one can identify the person who makes each remark. It is impossible to do this from the tape alone. A third observer, then, must jot down an identification number for the person speaking and the first few words of his remarks. The typist can then very easily attribute each comment to the proper person. (Later, real names are changed to pseudonyms.)

The presence of three very busy observers taking rapid notes at the end of the conference table would be extremely distracting to the members of a committee. In the small groups laboratory, these observers are behind a one-way mirror some eight to ten feet from the center of the table, facing its open end. The immediate distraction consists, then, of a mirror reflecting the group; a secondary distraction is the subject's consciousness that persons behind the mirror are watching. While this is an unusual situation for the group to be in, we must compare the distractions involved here with those of operating in the open presence of the observers. For example, on at least two occasions in the laboratory meetings someone swore, the members laughed, and the profanity was corrected for the benefit of the observers—but the same thing occured at least twice also in the field when I operated a tape recorder at real meetings.

How can the effects of the one-way mirror observation be minimized? One way is to pretend it does not exist. This was attempted with our pretest group: the members of the committee were ushered into the laboratory and told off-handedly that there were observers

---

[18]Robert F. Bales, *Interaction Process Analysis* (Reading, Mass.: Addison-Wesley, 1950).

[19]The Bales categories are detailed in Appendix A.

watching but that they should be ignored and the group should proceed with its tasks. The result was appalling. Instead of discussing their own decision, the subjects lectured the hidden observers in this fashion: "As you very well know, Sam, in the town of. . . ." And at one point a subject brought his irritation out into the open: "I like to see the people I'm talking to."

As a result of this experience, the procedures were changed. Each group was given a guided tour of the observation areas, shown the tape recorder (but not the Bales moving tape machine, which listed such categories as "tension release" and "shows antagonism" on the front), introduced to the observers, and told they would be taking notes. In contrast to the pretest group, subsequent groups turned their attention quickly to their own tasks, apparently oblivious of the observers.

INTRODUCING AN EXPERIMENTAL ELEMENT

The techniques described above do not constitute an experiment in the strict sense. The procedures were not varied from group to group; thus we must depend primarily on inferences drawn from *post hoc* comparisons within groups and among groups and individuals. This approach is consistent with the hypothesis-generating, primarily observational purposes of the research. However, it is possible to introduce certain experimental elements without disrupting radically the "reality" of the committee meeting. Disruption is minimized if the experimental stimulus introduced is one which the group experiences from time to time in its regular procedures. For example, if we were interested in the effects of the presence of reporters on committee processes, we might bring a reporter into a meeting at the half-way point. Or new information might be fed to the group after it had reached a preliminary decision. These are not infrequent occurrences in the regular course of committee work. On the other hand, the introduction of some strange procedure, such as adding stooges to investigate the effects of changes in group size, could be expected to throw the committee off balance.

In order to test certain hypotheses about the role of the chairman, I decided to see what would happen when the group was left without him for a brief period. That is, if the chairman is performing certain important functions, these functions should lapse or be taken over by someone else when he leaves. Therefore, at exactly fifteen minutes after the second task began, I called the chairman out into the hall for a five-minute conversation. The five-minute period was used to clear up some questions about the form and content of the board's budget.[20] The chairman was then returned to the meeting for the remainder of the task.

This event did not appear to suprise either the chairman or the other members of the group. In their regular meetings, it occasionally happens that the chairman is called out for a telephone call or a brief discussion about some pressing matter. The disruption, in other words, is in some sense a normal disruption.

ESTIMATING THE IMPACT OF THE LABORATORY

My *impression,* like that of many other researchers,[21] is that the real group in the laboratory quickly becomes accustomed to the situation and directs its attention to the task at hand. The members pore over their budgets, ask each other questions, use their own jargon, and argue and joke in an apparently natural manner. Furthermore, it is *plausible* to suppose that they would do so, given their past history, the familiar tasks, the members' limited acting abilities, and the known tendency for personal styles and patterns of interpersonal relations, once established, to persist.

For hard evidence on the impact of the laboratory, we must wait for careful comparative studies based on observations of the same committees in the field and in the laboratory. This we do not have. But some evidence is available, of three sorts:

1. Decision Evidence. Here we can compare the content of the committee's decisions in both settings, on the hypothesis that they would be consistent. For example, as mentioned above, the boards of finance which had been engaged in running conflict with their school boards over recent years "adopted" more restrictive measures in the laboratory than did the boards with more harmonious histories.

2. Process Evidence. Are the most active members at home also the most active in the laboratory, and the usually inactive also inactive there? Does the group exhibit about the same degree of conflict and harmony in the laboratory as at home? Five of the boards of finance kept accurate enough minutes of their regular meetings to make a rough participation count possible. In four of these five cases, the top participator in the laboratory was one of the top two participators at

---

[20]All scores for the chairman, both as initiator and receiver, were subsequently adjusted to compensate for this period.
[21]Cf. Lindzey, I, 399; and George C. Homans, *The Human Group* (New York: Harcourt, Brace, 1950), p. 53.

home; in four of the five cases, the person who participated least in the laboratory was one of the two participating least back home.

The twelve boards which met in the laboratory were not recorded in their home settings, but eleven other boards were. Five decision-making sequences were selected from these field tapes. A comparison of their over-all Bales scores shows a pattern fairly similar to that of the laboratory groups. The "positive" and "negative" categories are broadly equivalent to agreement and disagreement; Bales calls them "social emotional" responses. Table I.1 shows that the laboratory groups were perhaps somewhat more restrained in these categories than were the groups at home. But the general patterns are quite similar.

TABLE I.1
Percentage of Interaction by Major Category,
for Excerpts from Field Recordings and Complete Laboratory Recordings

Bales Categories	Percentage of Interaction	
	Field	Laboratory
Positive (1,2,3)	17%	12%
Answers (4,5,6)	63	72
Questions (7,8,9,)	9	7
Negative (10,11,12)	11	9
Total	100 (N = 1,229)	100 (N = 13,593)

In their questionnaires, the laboratory subjects were asked to choose between the following alternatives (F4), as composed by William G. Schutz[22]:

G

When I am with a group of people I ordinarily don't try to participate very much. I almost always sit back and listen to what the others say much more than I talk. When I do talk it is usually just a sentence or two. I rarely make a very long contribution. Also most of the time I respond to some-one else's question rather than initiat-ing anything on my own. Perhaps I don't participate in groups as much as I should.

H

When I am with a group of people I try to take a very prominent part. I almost always try to be in the lime-light. I don't like to remain silent very long and almost always try to get into the thick of a discussion before long. Sometimes I even say something startling, partly to get recognized. For whatever reason I am almost always one of the highest participators in any group. Perhaps I even overdo it some-what.

[22]*FIRO: A Three-Dimensional Theory of Interpersonal Behavior* (New York: Holt, Rinehart and Winston, 1960), p. 224. FIRO is quoted in this book with the kind per-mission of Dr. Schutz. Parenthetical references are to the questionnaires in Appendix C.

Circle the answer that best describes
the way you really act and feel.

I AM MUCH MORE LIKE G THAN I AM LIKE H [1]	I AM SOMEWHAT MORE LIKE G THAN I AM LIKE H [2]	I AM SLIGHTLY MORE LIKE G THAN I AM LIKE H [3]
I AM SLIGHTLY MORE LIKE H THAN I AM LIKE G [4]	I AM SOMEWHAT MORE LIKE H THAN I AM LIKE G [5]	I AM MUCH MORE LIKE H THAN I AM LIKE G [6]

The question refers, it should be noted, not to participation in the laboratory but to one's usual group participation. Table I.2 shows, for respondents choosing each of the above answers, the ratios of the mean number of their laboratory interactions to the group mean in total interaction initiated in the laboratory. These bits and pieces of evidence support the idea that there is at least a rough similarity between the board's interaction in its natural setting and that in the laboratory.

TABLE I.2
Reported Usual Participation and Laboratory Participation

Usual Participation (as reported by respondents)	Laboratory Participation (mean ratio to group mean)
6 (High)	1.64 (N = 7)
5	1.20 (N = 8)
4	1.24 (N = 13)
3	.87 (N = 18)
2	.69 (N = 16)
1 (Low)	.86 (N = 20)

3. Reports by the Members. Perhaps the most obvious way to estimate the extent and nature of the laboratory's impact is to ask the members about it. In the questionnaires, they were asked, "To what extent did the members act in the discussions today as they usually act in board meetings?" (Q3) The responses are shown in Table I.3.

If the laboratory experience had radically altered group behavior patterns, the members would, I believe, have said so. However, their answers may be deceptive when we are trying to estimate less extensive changes: after all, the participants were *supposed* to act as they did at home.

TABLE I.3
Respondents' Estimates of Similarity of
Laboratory Meetings to Usual Meetings

Estimates of Similarity	
Exactly the same	54%
Very nearly the same	37
Somewhat the same	6
Very different	0
Completely different	0
N/A	2
Total	99 (N = 85)

Another finding rests on firmer evidence. Content analysis of the typed transcripts included a count of all references to the laboratory, the researchers, observers, microphones, mirrors, and so on, which were made during the task sessions when the board was "alone" in the room. The results are displayed in Table I.4.

TABLE I.4
Frequency of References to Laboratory Situation,
in Tasks Number 1 and Number 2

References to Laboratory Situation as a Percentage of S's Total Referents	*Percentage of S's*
None	59%
0.1% − 1.0%	31
1.1 − 1.5	7
1.6+	4
	101 (N = 85)

Here again, if the impact of the laboratory had been very intense, we would perhaps expect more conversation about it — more references to "what they want us to do" or "working under these conditions." The subjects' silence on this matter does not, of course, prove that they were not thinking about it.

Finally, we can observe how the members react directly to the experimenter.[23] If they experienced a great deal of tension due to the instructions and conditions of the day, we might expect these outspoken adults to express a certain irritation or antagonism toward me

[23]In his article, "A Sleeper Variable in Small Groups Research: The Experimenter," *Pacific Sociological Review,* V (1962), 21-28, Theodore M. Mills presents a convincing case for incorporating the experimenter and his relations with the group into research design and interpretation. See also R. Rosenthal and K. Fode, "The Effect of Experimenter Bias in the Performance of the Albino Rat," *Behavioral Science,* VIII (1963), 183-89.

during the afternoon evaluation session at the end of the day. If, on the other hand, they were cowed by the whole experience, we might expect them to agree with nearly everything I had to say. The Bales scores enable us to check these suppositions. In fact, in this research the members' comments to me were heavily concentrated (to me: 94.4 per cent; to one another: 78.7 per cent) in the Question and Answer categories (Bales Nos. 4, 5, 6 and Nos. 7, 8, 9) rather than the Positive and Negative categories (Bales Nos. 1, 2, 3 and Nos. 10, 11, 12). And they agreed with me about 3.3 times as often as they disagreed with me, compared with a ratio of 1.9 for their agreement and disagreement with one another. The indication is, first, that the members reacted to me in a businesslike way and, second, that they perhaps showed some tendency to be extra agreeable with me. The effects are not extreme ones; the general picture does not support the conclusion that real officials would be very disturbed or angry at being manipulated in an experimental way.

Once again, the data are only suggestive. A sophisticated critic might suggest that the subjects were repressing their intense feelings of antagonism. Such an interpretation seems unnecessarily complicated: if they were quite irritated, they would have shown it.

TYPES OF EFFECTS

Given the small number of participants who reported differences between their laboratory meeting and their regular meetings, it is difficult to determine the detailed nature of or reasons for such differences as were noted. Breakdowns become progressively less meaningful as the N in each cell dwindles. I mention here the minor indications that do occur, recognizing that changes in a few answers would alter them radically. In the first place, members from the smaller towns seem to have been more aware of differences than were members from large towns, as Table 1.5 shows.

Secondly, members who report spending "most" or "all" of their time in their main occupation "talking with others" (Q49), are more likely to have seen the laboratory meeting as "exactly the same."

And members who rank being "very well liked" as more desirable than being "a leader" or "prominent in the activities" (F5D) are less likely to have seen the laboratory meeting as exactly the same as their usual meetings.

These hints point in the direction common sense would also take us: that people who move in a more cosmopolitan environment, who are accustomed to ready verbalization, and who are not overly con-

TABLE I.5
**Percentage of Respondents Reporting Laboratory "Exactly the Same,"
by Town Population Category**

Town Population Category	Percentage Reporting "Exactly the Same"
Four large towns Population range: 30,000 – 46,200	68% (N = 28)
Four medium-sized towns Population range: 7,300 – 19,500	52% (N = 29)
Four small towns Population range: 1,200 – 2,900	46% (N = 26)

TABLE I.6
**Percentage of Respondents Reporting Laboratory "Exactly the Same,"
by Frequency of Occupational Talk**

Reported Proportion of Occupational Time Spent Talking	Percentage Reporting "Exactly the Same"
All or most	61% (N = 57)
Less	42% (N = 26)

TABLE I.7
**Percentage of Respondents Reporting Laboratory "Exactly the Same,"
by Desire to Be "Very Well Liked"**

Rank Given to "Being Very Well Liked"	Percentage Reporting "Exactly the Same"
First	41% (N = 34)
Second or third	63% (N = 46)

TABLE I.8
**Percentage of Respondents Reporting Differences between
Laboratory Meetings and Usual Meetings**

Kind of Difference	Percentage Reporting
Problems more artificial (not "real")	12%
Time restricted	9
Being observed	9
Other responses (e.g., Lack usual information, etc.)	11
No differences noted	59
Total	100 (N = 85)

cerned with whether others like them or not, are more likely to move into the laboratory situation with a minimum of disturbance.

To get at some of the particular kinds of effects the laboratory setting had on board members, I asked them two open-ended questions: "What were some of the differences between today's meeting and your usual meetings, in the ways members acted?" and "What were the reasons for these differences?" (Q4,5) The questions elicited similar answers, which could be combined and coded as in Table I.8.

Carrying the analysis further gets us into very small numbers indeed. There are very minor indications that members who are relatively low in education but high in self-designated social class are more likely to report "being observed," and that the college-educated, of whatever class, are more apt to note the artificiality of the problems or the time restrictions.

The general picture which emerges from these bits and pieces of evidence on the impact of the laboratory setting upon a committee meeting can be summarized in one long sentence. For the local government committee, the impact is not overwhelming; it may be quite moderate, and it is probably about what we would expect—that is, there are discernible effects due to the hypothetical nature of the tasks, the time limitations, and the presence of observers; and these effects tend to be more intense for the small town committeemen, for those who talk little in their regular work, and for those who are relatively more sensitive to other people's reactions.

THE "TYPICAL" MEMBER AND THE FLAVOR OF DISCUSSION

Before proceeding to the substantive results, it may be useful to bring clearly to mind a picture of the "typical" participant in the research and to depict the way the groups went about their deliberations in the laboratory. The characterization of a hypothetical "typical" member is based on averages and frequencies drawn from questionnaire replies, and it omits the finer shadings of intensities and meanings, thus obscuring variations from group to group. Furthermore, we have no control group of non-members. Consequently, "high" and "low" scores may or may not represent answers specific to the boards of finance members. Keeping these qualifications in mind, we can then tentatively characterize the typical participant.

He is fifty-three years old, has had two years of college, and now makes about $14,500 a year, before taxes. He sees himself as middle or upper-middle class. When he was a child, he reports, his parents paid a good deal of attention to him, combining warm affection with strict discipline. They were moderately interested in politics, and both belonged to the same political party which he now prefers. He has lived in his town 29 years and has taken an active part in civic organizations and party affairs. He is not a member of his party's town committee, but considers himself a strong party supporter. Personally, he has no particular political ambitions, having given little thought to the idea of running for full-time office. Democratic versus Republican differences, he believes, are more evident in their candidates and party members than in their principles and their stands on issue.

The typical member's occupation gives him a good deal of personal satisfaction. It involves much conversation and frequent conferences. He expects his income to rise over the next ten years. A social person, he enjoys an evening with friends at least once a week. More of his friends are active in civic organizations and community social affairs than in government or political parties. He visits with other board members occasionally, but not "very often."

About three years ago, he was asked to become a member of the board of finance. He had never run for election or held an appointive office, but accepted the call out of a sense of duty and an interest in local issues. Membership on the board has since become very important to him, although he does not consider it *the* most important activity he has ever engaged in. He rates the board's performance high, thinks the public and other town officials also rate it high, and would be willing to serve at least two more terms in the future. He feels that he has done at least a fair job as a member, and that he exercises more influence on the board's decisions than most other members do. Generally he does not hesitate to disagree with other members — he feels others are more likely to find him too opinionated than too indecisive. The chairman, he thinks, should take a strong hand in conducting meetings, and not just stick to routine presiding. He feels the board has managed to keep town expenses on an even keel.

The typical member is definitely conservative. He would rather not see his son go into politics, and takes a dim view of political deals. In his town, he reports, a small group of people make most of the important decisions. The main goal of town government should be to encourage community growth, especially in commerce and industry, he believes — and he believes that most of the other board members would agree with him. On the other hand, he thinks that most citizens would stress the goal of creating a pleasant, comfortable, and safe environment for community residents.

There is no more a "typical" discussion than a "typical" member, but perhaps it may help to set the scene if we "listen" to one board as it works in the laboratory on a budgeting problem:

MEMBER 4: Joe, I'd like to go back to my way of thinking – in fact, right now, I would point out, when you get this hypothetical question – the police department. We allocated $5000 for traffic and safety surveys.

CHAIRMAN: What page is that?

M4: Page 14 F.

(Shuffle of papers)

M4: It's budget 14, but 14 F is where the breakdown is. It says page 3, 14 F – down at the bottom of the page.

CHAIRMAN: What is the number, Dan?

M4: 545. There's a $5000 item there for traffic survey and perhaps we could allocate $4000 for the traffic survey and they could go ahead with the traffic survey as they requested. And if they find that they're running out of funds they could always come to the board during the year for an additional allocation or perhaps while their budget – while they are operating their budget, if they find they are not hiring the men that they were going to hire, or they can't obtain them as fast as they've got them budgeted for, and they haven't gone over in their running budget during the year for salaries, they can refund –

M1: You can't take money out of salaries –

M7: Well, Dan, look, now that's –

M1: – come back into the budget –

CHAIRMAN: May I ask you fellows to speak one at a time, so we can –

M4: I'll just say one more thing. In other words, I'm talking about a transfer within the department. If they find themselves strapped for that $1000, which I'm sure they can do, because it's done every year in various departments.

CHAIRMAN: Well, we tried to keep this in mind, anything which has to do with the salaries and so forth, in a class by itself.

M1: That's right.

CHAIRMAN: In other words, we try not to go away from that. I mean we stick pretty much to that, usually we don't transfer from that at all.

M4: Well, I'm saying if it's – I'm not talking about salaries themselves, I'm talking about, for example, we give them at the beginning of the year additional men. Now these additional men are not hired for three or four months, sometimes five months, sometimes they run into difficulty where they can't get replacements, so they've got that unexpended balance so that if an emergency arose they could transfer that unexpended balance to this $1000 we're reducing their traffic survey.

M1: I think he's making two moves in order to get one move we have to have. He's making two moves – he's moving out of the contingency of the police department and now we're turning around and taking more to put it back in where that department needs it. So I don't see why you take a chance on two moves, if we can't take it

on one move, and that's the only thing they're doing. I recommend that we go to the public works department — $652,000.
CHAIRMAN: What page is this?

And so on. We shall return from time to time to excerpts from the discussion transcripts, some of them rather more sparkling than the above. But this provides some indication of the general development of discussion as the board explores various alternatives. (Eventually an entirely different solution was decided upon.) From this kind of raw data it is possible to derive some tentative conclusions as to the central criteria employed by these particular committees in performing their central function — budgeting.

CHAPTER II

Budgeting: Who Gets What and Why

ASK THE AVERAGE congressman or senator what three committees he would like to be on and the answer is very likely to include appropriations. Government officials at all levels eventually come to recognize that pervading power in all its myriad forms, shaping large and small decisions, stimulating here and depressing there, reflecting the past power structure and determining that of the future, there is a common element: money. If not the root of all political evil or the manure of all political good, money is at least the sap of government. The most grandiose program, deprived of adequate nourishment, withers and dies; the smallest branch of government, stimulated by a generous flow of capital, may blossom beyond all expectation.

Thus, to focus attention on the institutions of government that decide when how much money will be spent, by whom, for what, is likely to illuminate a variety of significant aspects of power. In the present study, we are fortunate in having data which lend themselves to the direct analysis of budgetary processes in local government. We need not rely entirely on what the participants say they do when they make budget decisions; we can listen as they go about their work, noticing the particular kinds of values and criteria they actually invoke. In this chapter, I shall try to pull together from the records of the deliberations of the boards of finance on their first laboratory task, budgeting, the kinds of criteria which appeared to govern their decisions. But some introductory theoretical considerations necessarily precede this analysis.[1]

[1]See V. O. Key, Jr., "The Lack of a Budgetary Theory," *American Political Science Review*, XXXIV (1940), 1137-44; Verne B. Lewis, "Toward a Theory of Budgeting," *Public Administration Review*, XII (1952), 42-54; and Aaron Wildavsky, *The Politics of the Budgetary Process* (Boston: Little, Brown, 1964), chs. 4, 5.

COMPLEXITY, SYNOPTICISM, INCREMENTALISM, AND THE REAL QUESTIONS

Potentially at least, budgetary decisions are immensely complex. They can involve calculations covering the entire range of detailed governmental functions and operations, from the chemistry of water purification to the psychology of social work. Aaron Wildavsky's examples from the congressional budgetary process — e.g., should more money be spent on studies of homopoiesis or lymphomatosis[2] — could be matched at the local level. Potential complexities also exist in coping with relations among levels of abstraction, in assessing the implications of past actions for future ones, and in applying ethical standards to uncertain choices. In Chapter III, I shall try to show how various ambiguities in these matters provide opportunities for power strategies. Here the point is that the most determined budgeter can never hope to take into account all the complexities implicit in the decisions he must make.

Consider the "ideal" budget-maker. He begins by surveying the goals of the community, ranking them in order of importance and determining the temporal priority of each in relation to the others. He bases this initial step on a comprehensive knowledge of his town's economic, political, historical, and ecological character, projected into the future by means of appropriate techniques. Then he proceeds to determine the best means to these ends, making a detailed analysis of each department's resources, operations, and plans. Finally, he allocates funds among these activities in accordance with the priorities previously established and the probabilities of various unforeseen contingencies.

This "synoptic ideal"[3] is obviously impossible to obtain in its pure form, but it is often held out as a goal to be approximated as nearly as possible. Budget-makers are advised to move in this direction, to take into account as many facets of the problem as they can. At its worst, such advice is simply exhortation to try hard and do better. Analysts of

---

[2]Wildavsky, p. 9.

[3]David Braybrooke and Charles E. Lindblom, *A Strategy of Decision: Policy Evaluation* (New York: Free Press of Glencoe, 1963), ch. 3. On synoptic versus incremental approaches, see also Charles E. Lindblom, "The Science of 'Muddling Through,'" *Public Administration Review*, XII (1952), 79-88; Yehezkel Dror, Charles E. Lindblom, Roger W. Jones, Mickey McCleery, and Wolf Heydebrand, "Governmental Decision-Making: A Symposium," *Public Administration Review*, XXIV (1964), 154-65; James W. Fesler, "Administration in the Federal Government," *Yale Papers in Political Science*, No. 6 (1963); and Rufus P. Browning, "Innovative and Non-Innovative Decision Processes in Government Budgeting," a paper delivered at the 1963 Annual Meeting of the American Political Science Association.

actual budget-making processes as they are performed from day to day by human beings in official positions have come forth with a radically different picture of the budget-maker. In fact, they report, budgeters operate incrementally by restricting their attention to very small segments of the total problem, comparing a few alternative marginal departures from the existing situation, and considering only what can be done with readily available resources. While this view can be offered as a strictly empirical observation, it can also be used to elaborate a series of recommendations.

However, to concentrate on the stark contrasts between the synoptic ideal and the incremental reality is perhaps to miss some real questions of practical importance. The interesting questions regarding budget-making practices are:

1. Matters of Degree. The alternatives are not incrementalism versus synopticism, but more-or-less incrementalism versus more-or-less synopticism. To what extent can (should) the budgeter take into account a somewhat broader range of calculations than he does? To what extent can (should) he devote more of his time to marginal calculations at the expense of large and long-range considerations?

2. Matters of Method. There are any number of ways to simplify an excessively complex problem. What are the implications of choice among these various possibilities? What particular intellectual devices can (should) the budgeter adopt?

3. Matters of Rationality. Decision-makers may pursue strategies for simplification largely consciously, with an awareness based on rational choice, or largely unconsciously, in accordance with unexamined habits or predilections. Cognitive complexity is a psychological problem, a source of strain, which can be resolved by inadvertance or design, accidentally or purposefully.[4] The data to be presented next bear on these questions, and I shall come back later to some possible answers.

BUDGETARY CRITERIA

As will be recalled, each board of finance spent approximately thirty minutes in the small groups laboratory on a budget-reducing task, looking over its own most recent budget figures to determine where and by how much the total could be cut if this were necessary. These deliberations were tape recorded and, subsequently, complete, typed

---

[4]On conscious versus unconscious decision rules, see Karl W. Deutsch, *The Nerves of Government* (New York: Free Press of Glencoe, 1963), ch. 6.

transcripts were prepared. To find out what criteria were actually employed as the members approved and rejected reductions, a content analysis of this material was performed. First, all comments which could be identified as favoring specific reductions were distinguished from those opposing specific reductions, giving totals of 559 and 420 respectively. Then these comments were assigned to categories meant to catch the main substantive content of each as this emerged inductively from the data. In Table II.1, the frequencies of these comments are detailed. These figures and a freer perusal of the transcripts cast light on several board of finance techniques for simplifying an extremely complex set of problems.[5]

TABLE II.1
Budgetary Criteria:
Percentage of Comments Expressing Reasons for
and against Proposed Reductions

Reasons for *Cuts*

Magnitude and Change of Expenditures	
Appropriation was increased in last budget	16.8%
New item	11.8
Large item	9.1
Account shows surplus; current expenditure rate	8.9
Subtotal	46.6
Effects on Operations	
Cuts will not hamper services	13.6
Expenditure can be postponed	8.9
Subtotal	22.5
Uncertainty	
Original appropriation based on rough estimate, was not considered carefully by BF	10.9
Funds may not be needed; can correct later	6.3
Subtotal	17.2
Other	
Effect on tax rate	4.7
Comparison with other departments	2.3
Probable public reaction to cut	1.6
Probable reaction of department to cut	1.3
Comparison with other towns	.9
Competence or sincerity of requester	1.3
Miscellaneous	1.6
Subtotal	13.7
Total	100 (N = 559)

[5]Many of these themes are similar to those Wildavsky found at the federal level. See Wildavsky, chs. 2, 3.

Reasons against *Cuts*		
Uncontrollable Items		
"Can't be touched"	27.4%	
State requirements	8.1	
Subtotal		35.5
Appropriation Already Minimal		
BF cut from last request	10.5	
BF considered last request carefully	9.1	
Appropriation has decreased	5.0	
Request was minimal; tight	4.3	
Subtotal		28.9
Effects on Operations		
Cut will hamper services	16.0	
Effect uncertain, perhaps harmful	7.4	
Urgent; cannot be postponed	.5	
Subtotal		23.9
Other		
Probable public reaction to cut	3.8	
Effect on tax rate	2.4	
Competence or sincerity of requester	2.1	
Probable reaction of departments	.2	
Comparison with other departments	0	
Comparison with other towns	0	
Miscellaneous	3.3	
Subtotal		11.8
Total		100.1 (N = 420)

Criterion 1: Controllability

The distinction between controllable and uncontrollable costs is a preliminary criterion, applied when the members of the board attempt to decide where to focus attention rather than how much to cut. Certain expenditures have been committed by previous long-range decisions, or are tied in closely with basic legal requirements, or are mandatory accompaniments of other fundamental costs such as retirement funds or wage levels. Excluding these from consideration enables the board to devote its efforts to those matters on which it has discretion in the short run. This is the most frequent of the reasons advanced against cutting particular items. Obviously it can be a useful device when it is consciously applied from the beginning.

In a good many cases, however, the reasons for categorizing an item as uncontrollable are not clear. The borderlines between expenses which are irrevocably committed, those which could be affected by changes in other areas of the budget, and those which are thought to be difficult to change without disrupting essential services are not well defined. Often the members seem to be referring not to some fixed commitment but to a general *consensus* among themselves that changing an item would be undesirable. Typically, the item is mentioned, someone comments that it "can't be touched," all quickly agree, and they pass on to the next item. In these cases ambiguities in the meanings of controllability are not consciously explored, and it is possible for many specific appropriations to drift over into the uncontrollable category.

Criterion 2: Size and Increase

Most boards appear to recognize that cutting budget requests "across the board" by some fixed percentage or amount is, in the long run, destructive of budgetary rationality. The lesson is learned through a series of feedback processes. Over the years, such flat cutting teaches the requesting agencies to anticipate losing a fixed proportion of their requests, regardless of the merits of the case, and thus to adjust the requests accordingly. The budget reviewers eventually catch on to this ploy and automatically deduct the traditional "fat" or excess before beginning their real cutting. The requester may then be motivated to pad even more, and so on. Eventually both sides begin to lose confidence in one another, and to realize how ridiculous the game is becoming. The spiral may end with mutual confessions of sin, prayers for forgiveness, and oaths of reform. Judging from comments offered in the boards of finance discussions, across-the-board cutting is passé.

Generally attention is fixed on the large items in the budget and those requests which have increased over the previous request and/or appropriation. Large requests indicate large and, thus, important programs and therefore, members conclude, large opportunities for savings. The focus is on agency *totals* as clues for the allocation of attention. This is the easiest way to distinguish among requests, and chopping down a large appropriation may pay off in money terms much more than many smaller-scale decisions.

There is, however, a hidden assumption in this line of reasoning which may be fallacious: that a large item contains roughly the same proportion of "fat" as the smaller items do—or perhaps more. This would be a valid conclusion if, for example, the requests were padded on a percentage basis, by adding, say, 10 per cent. But otherwise the following proposition would probably hold for most departments: the larger the request, the more times it has been carefully reviewed during the request-making process. The board of education budget, almost always the largest single item, has filtered up to the board of finance through a long series of preliminary stages: teachers, principals, super-intendent of schools, board of education budget committee, and full board of education. The tree warden, on the other hand, may bring his comparatively small but unreviewed request directly to the board of finance. Insofar as each successive review tends to reduce initial estimates, many large final totals may indicate budgetary muscle rather than fat.

The technique of concentrating on the large items, then, may be undertaken consciously, but it is often practiced without complete awareness of critical assumptions.

But, in fact, the board of finance may make few comparisons from department to department on the basis of size or any other principle. The main procedure in practice is to consider the budget *horizontally* — this year versus last year — rather than *vertically* — Department A versus Department B. Increased requests stand out; sometimes the difference between last year's and this year's request is calcu-lated and entered on the budget forms in order to highlight this aspect. The operative assumption seems to be that stable expenditure levels are *prima facie* valid and need not be closely examined, while raises are suspicious and need detailed scrutiny. As a simplifying device, this technique reflects the much more general tendency for a person to notice objects in motion amidst a collection of fixed objects.

However, designating what is moving and what is still depends on a further specification: moving in relation to what? A *stable* or constant money figure may conceal marked instability in the level of services rendered, in real expenditure terms (considering prices), in changes in the revenue side of budgeting, and so forth. A *raise* in the salary schedule of 2 per cent a year represents a *decline* in real incomes if the cost of living is going up 3 per cent a year. If more state funds are made available for road work, a *stable* figure for the town highway depart-ment in fact represents an *increase*. In periods of increased welfare needs, as in a recession, a *stable* welfare expenditure conceals an actual *drop* in spending per case. Thus simplification by means of concentration on departures from previous spending levels risks distor-tion and substantive error in the budget. If most other conditions are stable, however, it offers one more way to cut down the burden of calculation.

Criterion 3: Concreteness

If asked to describe their procedures in budgeting, most members of the boards of finance would, I believe, refer to the above techniques in one form or another. The budgeter is usually aware that he uses such techniques — these are the reasons which he advances overtly. But frequently there is an aspect of each technique of which he remains unconscious: the bases for the reasons which he advances are seldom explored and, I think, seldom thought about. The remaining criteria to be discussed fall largely in the latter category of simplification techniques employed unconsciously, or at least according to no regular design

When a person must make a decision in an ambiguous situation, he searches for some familiar element or set of elements with which he has had much experience, and concentrates on that. In a discussion of education, for example, the philosopher is apt to focus on the general goals, the psychologist on the learning process, and the economist on the marginal utility of various resource allocations. Board of finance members often bring to their official tasks considerable experience in practical affairs, gathered over years of business activity. This means that they are familiar with budgets and can quickly grasp the practical implications of budgetary details. But these very strengths may divert attention toward the concrete, down-to-earth details of a problem and away from certain less tangible but relevant matters.

Take the recreation budget, for example. Questions such as what variety of fencing is best for a playground, what it is reasonable to pay for grading a ball field, and the like are quite similar to those encountered in the course of business. But other matters of key import to the recreation program seem strange: Which of several alternative teen-age sports programs would contribute most to the health and welfare of the youngsters? What balance should be struck between programs for the various age groups? These kinds of questions are in fact decided by the ways the board allocates funds. But they may be answered indirectly, without discussion or adequate information, because of the board's tendency to wrestle with physical details rather than policy alternatives. Many of the comments scored above as effects on operations are of this nuts-and-bolts variety.

Criterion 4: Immediacy

The pressure to keep the discussion in board meetings focused on the here and now is intense. Exaggerated in the laboratory situation, scarcity of time is a problem also in the normal budget deliberations, as the deadline for completing the budget approaches inexorably. The member who brings up the long-range picture, or who reaches too far back into the past for his illustrations, may be made to feel that he is interrupting an emergency meeting to introduce irrelevancies. This year's problems are bad enough without adding in those of a decade hence. Simplification is thus achieved by restricting attention to the present and near future.

Yet, of course, decisions made in the immediate context do shape long-run community developments. This is especially evident in large capital expenditures. When a bridge is built in a certain location, the town is, in effect, committed for years to come to a certain pattern of traffic flow in that area. Other land uses are excluded for a long time. Long-term effects on real estate values, business fortunes, and the like may be fixed. Attitudes expressed in the board of finance deliberations regarding community planning agencies often discount these implications but they cannot disprove them.

Viewing time in the other direction, if the board focuses only on what is immediate, it tends to eliminate much relevant evidence from the past. This is not to reintroduce all the complications which simplification techniques are meant to handle, but only to point out that there may be particular decisions upon which particular past experiences might bear, and that an unconscious decision to exclude from consideration everything that happened before last year may not be entirely reasonable. The key problem is one of information retrieval or feedback. Some relevant historical information will be stored in the minds of the members and they may be motivated to introduce it, but the imposition of group restraints on such expressions excludes this vital resource. Other information might be kept in systematic written form, readily available for reference when needed.

Here again, then, a device for simplifying complexity bears with it the possibility of introducing unnecessary additional complexities, as the same problems are encountered and muddled through again and again, without benefit of ordered hindsight.

We have negative evidence of another variety of immediacy or insularity as a criterion: the rather surprising lack of reference to experiences in other towns. The members of a board of finance focus on their own community almost exclusively. Fewer than 1 per cent of the comments favoring cuts and none of those opposing cuts refer to comparisons with other towns. In part this is a result of lack of information, few boards being aware that comparative statistical data on town budgeting decisions are readily available. In part it reflects community pride—"Ours is a unique town"—and in part reasonable doubts about the transferability of findings from one setting to another.

But among the 169 towns in Connecticut there are undoubtedly many which face similar problems in education, law enforcement, municipal financing, and so on. The small town of Bethlehem may gain little enlightenment from the teeming city of Bridgeport, but it might profit from a look toward Canaan or Bozrah or Hebron.

Criterion 5: Uncertainty

All of these criteria could be considered methods for reducing uncertainty. In a more complex way, however, the boards appear to use the certain-uncertain distinction itself as a simplifying device. We notice in Table II.1 such items as "Original appropriation, based on rough estimate, was not considered carefully by BF," "Funds may not be needed; can correct later," "BF considered last request carefully," "Effect uncertain, perhaps harmful." The thrust of these comments seems to be that at any given time the board will (*a*) not reconsider decisions about which the members have been certain in the past, and (*b*) make new decisions, without feeling entirely certain about them, only if such decisions can be taken tentatively and any ill effects can be corrected later. The latter gambit is a prediction that in some cases (usually those involving small expenditures) risks can be progressively eliminated on the basis of future feedback. For example, most towns can expect to encounter sudden needs for additional snow removal funds from time to time, and to draw on various contingency funds to meet these needs as they arise. Money for hiring new school teachers, on the other hand, is needed once and for all near the first of the year in order to complete contractual arrangements. This invites gambling a bit with the snow but taking a cautious approach with the teachers.

The retrospective dimension of uncertainty as a criterion is somewhat simpler. The board looks back at its prior deliberations and recalls that in some cases decisions were made with considerable confidence and in others with considerable doubt. The more uncertain they were, the more willing they are to reconsider. On the surface this appears to be an obvious and reasonable way to proceed, but it is open to at least one kind of irrational inference. That is, estimates of past certainty may be based almost entirely on past effort — on the time and energy previously devoted to reviewing a request. Members seem to feel that if a problem was initially considered at great length the solution was very likely right, or at least that new deliberations on the problem are unlikely to improve the solution. In many cases this makes sense, but in others the fact that much effort went into the making of a decision may indicate that members had many doubts, that many contingencies had to be taken into account, and/or that opinions had to be substituted for missing information. In other words, effort expended is sometimes, but not always, an accurate index of results achieved.

Criterion 6: Dollars and Cents

Another way to simplify the complexity of a decision is to focus on its formal details—in this case, the figures on the pieces of paper at hand. The numbers provide the fundamental basis for calculation, the expression of wants and costs in comparable monetary units. And arithmetic furnishes the fundamental techniques for comparing this program with that one, this year with last year, and so on.

The danger inherent here is that of falling into a kind of symbolic reification in which the representation is cognitively detached from the thing represented, the link between symbol and reality forgotten. In budgeting it is possible to become so absorbed in dollars-and-cents calculations that one loses track of what the figures stand for. This problem arises especially when a great deal of time is spent on arithmetic in order to bring together a coherent set of requests. The numbers come to have a life of their own as they are summed and subtracted and divided. This can lead to mistakes in emphasis and interpretation; for example, a decision to cut a request from one department by a certain amount may be treated as a precedent of sorts for cutting another department by the same amount. The forest is lost sight of as the trees fall all around.

These six criteria for simplification in budgeting—

1. Controllability
2. Size and increase
3. Concreteness
4. Immediacy
5. Uncertainty
6. Dollars and cents

—appear to be the main ones employed by the boards of finance. Of course, any aspect of budgeting not attended to suggests a technique for reducing complexity—for instance, little attention is paid to revenue-raising problems or to public opinion in these deliberations—but these half-dozen criteria seem to shape budgeting most determinatively. They bring us back to the "real questions" raised earlier.

Close study of the discussion transcripts leads to the conclusion that if these boards err, it is not in the direction of the "synoptic ideal."

We come away with the impression that far too little attention is devoted to the broader, longer-range implications of the decisions being made, and that evidence which could be highly useful is systematically ignored.[6] The temptation is strong to preach the gospel of the bigger picture, to urge more effort on all fronts. But this is unlikely to increase the effectiveness or rationality of the budgetary process. More to the point are considerations of how simplification can be accomplished without sacrificing so much of the larger dimensions of budgeting.

INCREMENTAL IMPROVEMENTS IN INCREMENTALISM

If the major problem for the budgeter is economizing his attention, then strategic decisions—those which subsume or predetermine some aspect of many lesser decisions—are of prime importance.[7] Strategic decisions pay off in savings in time and energy as the same types of problems come up repeatedly. For example, once a man decides to shave every morning, he need not concern himself further with the matter. The time taken to make this decision represents a saving, not a waste, of effort. The rule need not be applied rigidly; there will be occasions for breaking it. But by concentrating attention for a while on a recurrent problem and resolving it, one conserves mental energies for years to come.

For the boards of finance, and perhaps for other budget-making bodies, three kinds of strategic decisions appear to offer the best possibilities. None is new, but they are unevenly attended to.

1. Basic Policy and Timing Decisions

By consciously devoting time early in the budget process to determining the boundaries between all controllable and all uncontrollable

[6]On the conservative tendencies of incrementalism, see John T. Lanzetta and Vera T. Kanareff, "Information Cost, Amount of Payoff, and Level of Aspiration as Determinants of Information Seeking in Decision-Making," *Behavioral Science,* VII (1962), 459-73; Randall B. Ripley, "Interagency Committees and Incrementalism: The Case of Aid to India," *Midwest Journal of Political Science,* VIII (1964), 143-65; and Vernon Van Dyke, *Pride and Power: The Rationale of the Space Program* (Urbana: University of Illinois Press, 1964), ch. 16.

[7]On strategic simplification, see Deutsch, pp. 251-52; and Thomas C. Schelling, "Bargaining, Communication and Limited War," in *The Strategy of Conflict* (New York: Oxford University Press, 1963), pp. 53-80. On similar simplification techniques in Congress, see Ralph K. Huitt, "Congressional Organization and Operations in the Field of Money and Credit," in William Fellner *et al.,* eds., *Fiscal and Debt Management Policies* (Englewood Cliffs, N.J.: Prentice-Hall, 1963), particularly pp. 436-40.

costs, setting general cost-of-living salary adjustments, and the like, these matters are removed from the agenda of many meetings on specific budget items. Similarly, paying attention early to long-range community planning can dispose of conflicts which might otherwise crop up repeatedly. Timing decisions, particularly setting a schedule for the submission and consideration of requests, can save many an hour's *ad hoc* discussion about what to do next. The simple matter of setting a definite time for meetings—especially for *ending* meetings—removes another set of unnecessary uncertainties. Such cross-cutting decisions on specific, clearly defined topics offer much better possibilities for improvement than vague discussions of general goals or theories of administration.

2. Information-Processing Decisions

Part of the problem here is simply that of creating and collecting information: keeping accurate minutes, requiring reports from operating agencies, gathering statistics on various facets of town finance. The more serious problems involve organizing and communicating available information for maximum utility in making individual decisions. For example, one of the boards of finance regularly has before it, at budget time, a breakdown of the appropriations to each department over the last decade, including the percentage of the total town budget spent annually by each. Standardized budget forms facilitate quick access to relevant comparisons. By setting up a system for training new members and for distributing agendas and pertinent documents to all members for study before they come together at the meeting, the board can save much collegial learning time. Again, the significant pay-off results from *deciding,* consciously and definitely, how information is to be created, stored, and retrieved.

3. Delegation Decisions

The possibilities of delegation are largely unexploited by most boards of finance. Yet it is evident that much relevant research could be farmed out to finance officers, department heads, and clerks. If a program budget, in which each requesting agency spells out in simple narrative form the main services rendered in the past year and the program for the next year, is submitted, the members of the board will not have to dig this information out of the requesters at joint meetings. Research and recommendations on long-term community trends can also be delegated. And perhaps the biggest saving in time could be accomplished by assigning simple calculation tasks to a clerk with a desk calculator. The man hours consumed by problems in simple arithmetic add up impressively in many boards.

These are, of course, matters of detail on which there can be valid disagreement. The point which needs to be stressed is that analysis of such methods offers better possibilities for the incremental improvement of incrementalism than does a focus on grand alternative models of decision-making. If the goal is rational efficiency in exercising the power of the purse, such mundane moves have much to recommend them. If the purpose is to attain a position of power in the framework of town government, other devices, to which I now turn, may be called for.

CHAPTER III

Committee Culture: Images of Power

WHEN THE MEMBERS of a board of finance speak of "power," they refer not to relations among themselves but to relations between their board as a unit and other units in the system. Within the board, as they see it, decision-making is a matter of invention, rational discussion, compromise, and eventual agreement on the best practical solution. The problem is one of logical persuasion, not control, of deliberation, not dominance. They are aware of power as a problem only when they think of the officials sitting around other tables and making decisions which profoundly affect their own.

Here, as elsewhere in the governmental system, power is markedly contextual in character. It is not an isolated, temporary phenomenon abstracted from the flow of life, but rather one aspect of a complex system of interpersonal relationships.[1] In the board of finance discussions four power contexts are significant.

1. The Historical Context

Power does not simply exist; it must be established and then maintained over a period of years. The current power configuration is a

[1]On the significance of contextual considerations in power analysis, see Robert A. Dahl and Charles E. Lindblom, *Politics, Economics and Welfare* (New York: Harper, 1953), chs. 3, 4, 12, 13; William R. Dill, "The Impact of Environment on Organizational Development," in Sidney Malick and Edward H. Van Ness, eds., *Concepts and Issues in Administrative Behavior* (Englewood Cliffs, N.J.: Prentice-Hall, 1962); Robert L. Peabody, *Organizational Authority* (Englewood Cliffs, N.J.: Prentice-Hall, 1964); and James D. Barber, ed., *Political Leadership in American Government* (Boston: Little, Brown, 1964), pt. III. Cf. Erving Goffman, *The Presentation of Self in Everyday Life* (Garden City, N.Y.: Doubleday, 1959).

product of historical development, beginning, for these committees, with the institutionalization of the board of finance. The formal act of allocating authority to a new agency is but the start of a power-building process. Those who had been performing the functions transferred to the new board relinquish their actual powers reluctantly — "not grudgingly, but gradually," as one board of finance member describes it. The first problem of power, then, is to get it, to win it; and this requires political maneuvering over an extended period. The second problem is to hold on to the power attained and, if possible, to increase it. Here again the historical context is of immense importance. The board operates in the present on the basis of certain assumptions about its power inherited from the past. A comparison between two of our boards highlights the significance of this dimension.

In the first town, the board of finance has been for a number of years embroiled in continual controversy, especially with the board of education. Relating the history behind this situation, a member explains that "the board of finance had lost their authority completely, over what they had before, and lost their standing in the community." Agencies whose requests had been reduced by the board simply got them reinstated by the representative town meeting, a "glorified debating society," composed of people selected "from a political standpoint" and lacking in "ability or knowledge or training or education or anything else." Other members agree with this analysis: "Yes, they're the ones that put this board of finance in disrepute." Wherever the real blame lies, this board must strive for power within an historical context of defeat and embarrassment. Put another way, they bear a reputation for powerlessness which can be overcome only by finding ways to establish a position different from that which they have inherited.

Another board enjoys a much more favorable situation, as its chairman recounts:

There was a guy who served on the board of finance as chairman fifteen or twenty, twenty-five years ago. Name was J. O. Jones. And his conduct on this Board affected Marty Shortworth, who was chairman before me, and affects my conduct today. And the participation of those men who had immense prestige in the community affects all of our conduct today, because we just hand down traditions. We don't do this audibly or by any manual implementation, but we just acquire from previous generations of boards of finance a habit, a custom, a perspective, an attitude. And it's a blessing to me personally that down to this very moment this tradition of independence and non-partisanship has survived today.

The success of this board — in terms of getting acceptance for the recommendations it makes — has been remarkable. Not all of this can be explained by a tradition of "independence and non-partisanship." For example, the community in which it operates has extremely high property values and, thus, an exceptionally favorable tax base. But, for whatever reasons, its reputation for success is an important resource for the maintenance of power in the present. More generally, the first "given" factor in the present power situation is the history of power — or powerlessness — which the board inherits and transmits.

2. The Technical Context

As we saw in the last chapter, the boards of finance operate within a context of considerable technical complexity. Typically their focus of attention is strongly directed toward the details of the budget and toward the physical realities represented therein. They feel called upon to master as best they can the critical facts, to digest and employ all the relevant information. They work in a fact-oriented environment; they operate on the implicit assumption that once the key facts are known the problem will be solved. Even though they recognize that the technical complexities are potentially overwhelming, they devote little attention in any systematic way to discussing general techniques for simplification, but rather invoke such *ad hoc* rules of evidence and inference as seem to fit each problem. The general characteristics of the technical context (already amply illustrated in Chapter II) are (1) that information is perceived as the primary resource for solving problems, (2) that relevant facts are unevenly distributed among the participants in the governmental system, and (3) that standards for evaluating and interpreting information are implicit, flexible, and vague.

3. The Context of Shared Powers

Few things gall the typical board member more than the limitations imposed on the board by higher authorities. Federal authorities set standards for the use of federal funds; the state government has almost total authority over its "agents," the towns. As a member says in regard to the board of education, "so many of the demands that they place upon us as a board of finance are more or less forced upon them by the state board of education," and "the board of finance would have no control over the state board of education." Within the community, a multitude of other committees and officials share overlapping powers with the board of finance, so that only very rarely can a decision be made without taking some other agency into prolonged consideration.

The lines of jurisdiction—once one moves beyond the simple formalities—are blurred and wavering, as all the ambiguities of such words as "approving," "reviewing," "recommending," and "determining" attest. The board must recalculate repeatedly the current configuration of power.

For all their complaints, board members accept this kind of shared power as a given factor in their operations. Repeated references to checks and balances ("We've got to have resistance there; you can't just go along with everything they want"), of mutual consent ("You can't dictate anything in there"), and of tolerance for dissent ("I may disagree with what you say but still, I'm like Voltaire, I think you have the right to say it")—these feelings reflect the realities of the operating relationships among agencies. The object of power calculations and strategies is thus not to establish complete dominance over other actors in the system, but to increase power at the margins. The struggle for power is a game played within the ground rules of pluralism, not a battle for total victory.

4. The Moral Context

The social context of power is a fact; all I mean to do in calling attention to the "moral" or philosophical context is to suggest that power strategies within a system of shared powers have to be rationalized. Of all the rules of the game, this is probably the most inclusive and pervasive one. For the participants, it means a constant attention to the invention, communication, and criticism of the *reasons* for pursuing particular strategies. Sometimes these explanations refer to the empirical network of causes and effects which the actors perceive; sometimes they involve references to "principles" of power. And quite frequently we find members explaining their stands on grounds of psychological assumptions—estimates of the motives, attitudes, and beliefs which other actors hold. The moral requirement they feel is to provide some kind of justification for their strategies, some communicable, hopefully persuasive, argument for choosing a particular strategy. Behind this requirement is the assumption that power has a purpose, that it is not a good thing *per se* but an instrument for the accomplishment of something beyond itself. We do not encounter many references in the form, "Our board can do this, therefore we should do this," but there are continual references to "the principles of power of a board," the "power they're entitled to," "the power we need to get the job done." Thus many of the statements quoted in a discussion of strategies could be coded simultaneously as (*a*) *descrip-*

tions of an existent state of affairs, and (*b*) *justifications* for taking some particular line of action with regard to that state of affairs.

Within these four contexts, the subjects consider a wide collection of possible power moves. Despite their variety, these moves can be categorized, for analytical purposes, under relatively few headings on the basis of the major variable being manipulated. In reality, of course, they are entwined in an almost infinite number of complex relationships.

To illustrate how interagency power moves are perceived and rationalized, we can turn to the second task performed in the laboratory: the "hot issue" regarding relationships between the board of finance and the board of education. The problem was introduced as follows (for the complete text, as given to the subjects, see Appendix B):

A community very similar to yours in another state is seeking your advice as to the best practical system for running their educational system.

This was followed by three "proposals," which would establish conditions of no control, partial control, and direct control by the board of finance over the board of education. Then the members were asked,

What proposal would your board advise? You may recommend one of the above systems, amend them, or develop a different proposal of your own.

THE PREMISES OF POWER

It is often said that he who poses the questions controls the answers. A committee's discussion of possible power moves will be shaped significantly by the way the problem of power is defined. For example, the question on relations with the board of education might be perceived in any of the following terms: What arrangement of power would have the best results for this community? Which arrangement stands the best chance of being implemented in practice? Which system would facilitate recruitment of the best talents? Who favors and who opposes each of the alternative possibilities? Which arrangement stands the best chance of surviving over the long run? Which system most nearly accords with established traditions and/or central principles? Which one promises to solve the most pressing problems of today?

In any single discussion many of these questions are likely to arise. But some crowd out others, and the criteria which come to dominate the deliberations point the way to certain conclusions. Two contrasting themes are illustrated in these quotations:

If there were no checks and balances, you might as well give them [the board of education] a blank check and go home.

There are evils under any system. It all depends on how it's administered and it depends on the type of people that are on various boards and so on. If you have poor people on any board, or if you have poor people in any position, you are going to get a poor job.

The first position was echoed in many comments throughout the discussions. Left to their own devices, the board of education would "run wild," "get out of hand," there would be "a run-a-way of taxes." The premise is that the school board "always wants, as we all do," and that it is only the checking influence of the board of finance which keeps the members of the school board from giving free rein to their "idealistic," "enthusiastic," and even "fantastic" desires. This idea is advanced, of course, to justify greater control by the board of finance over board of education budgets. It defines the question, "How can we most effectively impose controls over a fundamentally irresponsible agency?" The solution is to invent ways to check them at every possible point.

The alternative position stresses the quality of board of education members and argues that harsh controls provide no solution. "Any system is dependent upon the people who are working in it"; "by and large I think we have a good board of education"; and, in any case, "that is something you can't legislate; that's dependent on the quality of your organization." The problem, then, is not how to maximize control over an adversary but how to insure smooth cooperation with a group of fundamentally decent people trying to do their job. In response to suggestions for unusual controls, the advocate of this position may say, "I believe the board of education would fall in line just as quick as any other department in town," when asked to conserve funds.

The conflict of premises here is fundamentally a question of motivations and attitudes. It results from differences in experience with the school board over the years and from more general perspectives regarding the motives of government officials. Not being philosophers, these officials do not pose the problem in terms of Hobbes versus Locke, but essentially they are shaping their decisions on assumptions about the nature of political man.[2] Particular questions regarding the appropriate character and strength of checks and balances get an-

[2]For many examples of the relevance of motives in intragovernmental relations, see Aaron Wildavsky, *The Politics of the Budgetary Process* (Boston: Little, Brown, 1964), pp. 74-84.

swered in this broader context: the pessimists (whose doubts rarely extend to estimates of their own qualities) want tight control, the optimists (pessimistic about the efficacy of regulations) would hold looser reins.

Once the general relevance of these motivational considerations is admitted, the question becomes one of interpretation: What rules of evidence should be applied? What particular circumstances are to be taken into account in determining how much control is justifiable? At least four types of arguments are advanced:

1. *Arguments based on the board of education's performance over a long period of years.* If on balance, taking into account occasional mistakes, their past record demonstrates responsibility and honesty, then additional controls are unnecessary and/or undesirable. Here the calculation is based on the other's *average* or typical behavior. Statements that "by and large," "traditionally," "generally speaking," the school board has been reasonable fall into this category.

2. *Arguments based on the current performance of the board of education.* In this case, the emphasis is often on the *trend* of their behavior: in the past they acted badly, but they have shown marked improvement in recent years. The implication usually drawn is that a few, relatively mild controls will suffice.

3. *Arguments based on particular incidents in the history of relations between the two boards.* Even though the average performance of past and present boards of education is rated favorably, single incidents may be invoked to show dangers which demand controls. The assumption is that the power relationships between the boards should be based on admittedly exceptional but *critical cases.* Usually advanced to justify more stringent controls, these arguments discard problems of sampling but retain an empirical element. The individual "horror stories" must be real ones.

4. *Arguments based on what the board of education is empowered to do, regardless of whether or not it has so acted in fact.* *Hypothetical cases* are brought forth to show what could happen or might happen unless further controls are implemented. Here the discussion is pushed away from considerations of evidence from the past and toward considerations of possibilities in the future.

There is, of course, no logically necessary reason why adoption of any one of these four positions on relevant evidence should imply a particular stance regarding the required degree of control. That is, average performance might be invoked to justify stringent controls, and hypothetical cases might be brought forward as arguments for freeing the school board from board of finance surveillance. But a survey of the discussion records indicates that in practice the case for controls is rarely buttressed by a broad overview of board of education behavior through the years, and the case for permissiveness rarely rests on hypothetical or critical cases. Our tentative prediction would be that the usual empirical relationships between rules of evidence and substantive conclusions will be those exemplified above, although the explanation for this pattern is obscure.

To illustrate how these different ways of defining the problem of power may affect decision-making, we can look at the course of the discussion in a board of finance which has had its share of difficulties with the board of education in recent years. The argument in progress concerns disparities between salaries paid to employees of the board of education and those of other town employees. Members 4 and 7 are in favor of restrictions to enforce comparable rates of pay; Members 1 and 5 come to the defense of the school board's autonomy.

> M4: . . . and your typist will be the same way, and your maintenance will be the same way—everything will just go right up, and the board of education will just go way out of line.
> M1: Well, I don't believe in that system at all. I believe the board of education would fall in line just as quick as any other department in town—
> M4: But they don't *have* to!
> M1: Wait a minute. They have their budget, but of course we have the say on the full amount that we will give them, and we can tell them what they will get—
> M4: In the department they can transfer any item they want.
> M1: No sir, no sir.
> M4: They don't have to bargain for it—
> M1: No sir—and there hasn't been any time that they've given the education and the school board [all they want].
>
> * * * * *
>
> M7: I'd like to see [greater control] as soon as we have the power to do it. We don't have the power to do it.
> M5: No, but if we had a closer relationship—we have a good, I think we have a good relationship with the board of education—
> M7: You're still talking about the relationship, but I'm saying that regardless of the relationship, they can do what they want, Joe.
> M5: Yeah, I know they can do what they want. I remember this particular point we discussed at length in our board of finance meeting.
> M7: Sure.

M5: As to Bill and also to Sam Williams, I think one year and the librarian —
M7: That year we cut each individual salary.
M1: That's right — we cut them, but they went back then and they raised them more than we wanted to give them, and then we should take and tell the townspeople or else keep our mouths shut.

* * * * *

M7: But if they work for the board of education, they can get any amount the board will give them.
M1: Wait a minute. They can get the amount the board of education submits to us —
M7: The hell they do, Mike.
M1: They do.
M7: They can get all they want.
M1: They do.
M7: They can give them $5000 if they want —
M1: No, they don't give them any more than what's appropriated.
M7: Oh, no, Mike, I know better.
M1: They'd never over-appropriate —
M4: What Charley is bringing out is that they *can* do it.
M1: They can't do it — you can't tell me — the board of education is as honest as any other department in town.

Out of this disjointed discussion the strong chairman eventually draws a compromise solution, employing arguments concerning both what *might* happen and what *has* happened. The interplay of various definitions of the situation is evident as Mike and Charley and Joe skip around from general characterizations, to critical cases, to hypothetical examples.

DEFINING FUNCTIONAL RELATIONSHIPS

The division of labor has power implications. On the face of it, various functions are assigned to various agencies of government in order to get a complex job done more efficiently. But the interdependence among agencies created by this division of labor inevitably produces conflict and, eventually, efforts to redefine responsibilities so as to gain a more favorable power position.[3] A basic problem in this struggle is *to enhance and protect one's power without sacrificing the*

[3]On functional interdependence and its power consequences, see Scott Greer, *Social Organization* (New York: Random House, 1955), pp. 19-21; James G. March and Herbert A. Simon, *Organizations* (New York: Wiley, 1958), ch. 5, especially p. 135; Norton Long, *The Polity* (Chicago: Rand McNally, 1962), ch. 6; and Gideon Sjoberg, "Contradictory Functional Requirements and Social Systems," *Journal of Conflict Resolution*, IV (1960), 198-208.

advantages of the division of labor. The objective is to avoid taking over the day-to-day, detailed work that others are doing, while gaining a vantage point for controlling the outcomes of their work. For example, a major disadvantage of Proposal C in the board of finance discussions, positing direct control over board of education budget items, was thought to be the "amount of detail," "the overwhelming job," "the tremendous job to say there shall be so many teachers in such and such a school." How can the other agency be controlled without taking on its work?

One way is to distinguish between "policy" and "administration." The board of finance is seen as an "independent," "outside," "objective" body representing the interests of the whole town and thus responsible for setting general guidelines for all other agencies, including the board of education. The strategic flexibility of this maneuver is due to the fundamental ambiguity of the distinction. Having asserted that "the board of finance ought to establish policy and not get into minutiae and forget the policy in trying to administer a program," a member can then go on to draw the line pretty much as he pleases. The decision to change textbooks every five years instead of every twelve years may be posed as a policy question and thus a proper topic for board of finance consideration. On the other hand, questions about the general purposes and basic methods of education (e.g., reading, writing, and arithmetic versus training in social adjustment) may be seen as specialized problems for the school board to handle under its own discretion. The variable to be manipulated here is the *level of generality* of decisions to be managed by one body or another.

A second recurring theme in the discussions is the distinction between "monetary" or "financial" control and control over the substance of decisions. For example:

M1: I think there should be some additional control added to this proposal to insure that children are being taught what we feel they should be taught in this country, even if we're wrong.

M7: John, you're bringing up the question of the school curriculum which was not one of these three questions. This is purely a question of financial control, not determining educational policy.

M1: Unfortunately, Jim, I don't feel that you can separate financial control and curriculum quality. I think that the two are tied so closely that once you delegate your responsibility to raise taxes and provide money for the board of education to professional educators, you must inevitably attract into that system people who have fixed ideas, they have axes to grind, and they're going to give your children what they think is best for them rather than

what you as a taxpayer feel they should be getting. I don't think
you can separate—

M7: Of course, under the law at present that is in the hands of board of
education to determine the educational policies of the school
system. Now, perhaps that should be changed. But it does seem
to me that we've got two separate things here. This question of
financial control is how we would control the board of education's
expenditures, but I don't think that the board of finance is in a
position to undertake to determine educational policies. . . .

CHAIRMAN: Isn't it true that these two concepts are always in conflict and that
the only answer, for practical operation of government, is a
compromise?

M1: Well, that is essentially the democratic process and that's what I
am in favor of, wholeheartedly.

CHAIRMAN: Against sin, too. (Laughter)

M1: These two conflicts coming together and arriving at a synthesis of
community opinion.

Here ambiguities regarding functional boundaries permit a
wide variety of interpretations. The argument to extend tighter control
over expenditures can be justified on the ground that this is well within
the special province of the board of finance and does not encroach on
the board of education's functional territory. Characterized more
broadly, the variable manipulated is the *medium* of decision. Similar
ideas are advanced from time to time by personnel officers, account-
ants, office-space allocators, purchasing agents, and other functional
specialists. The right to control some particular medium of decision
throughout the system is asserted without accepting the much wider
implications inherent in such control. "Monetary matters—that's all
we're deciding," says one member, arguing for restricting the board of
education.

A third way of manipulating functional definitions might be called
"nibbling around the edges." Any agency with a modicum of autonomy
performs (*a*) certain relatively distinctive central functions, and also (*b*)
many peripheral, supportive ones, such as housekeeping, recordkeep-
ing, maintenance of supplies and equipment, which are also performed
in other agencies. Control over these peripheral functions can be
asserted on grounds of economies of scale, the need for comparability
in pay rates and working conditions, and for any number of other
reasons. Such control circumscribes the *scope* of the other's decision-
making authority, reserving only the most central and distinctive
functions to the other's discretion. For example:

M4: We're not educators. We don't know their needs—they know
their needs. We don't know their systems—they know their

systems. But I would like to see, in Jack's line of thought, some kind of amendment whereby the non-professional salaries would come under the scope [of the board of finance] —

M7: And administrative —

M4: And the administrative — well, non-professionals in other words. I'm not talking about the teachers — leave the teachers out of this completely.

M7: I'm including the superintendent.

Here, and in other discussions, the move to "take away from the board of education non-educational functions" operates to reduce the scope of their decision-making — usually on the ground that this will free them to concentrate on their central functions. It is easy to see how thoroughgoing changes in this direction could reduce the other agency to impotence.

A much more radical manipulation of functional scopes — a solution considered seriously by seven of the twelve boards but adopted by none of them — would move strongly in the other direction. The school board would be freed from any control by the board of finance, made responsible for levying and collecting its own taxes and expending its own funds. According to advocates of this plan, the result would be a strong public reaction against "runaway" education expenses. The board of education would "have to stand on its own two feet" and "really fight for its items."

M4: ... Perhaps if the sole responsibility was theirs they might change their sights on some of this money they claim they need.

M7: I think you've got a good point there. I think that the taxpayer would eventually take care of that problem because once his school taxes got so high he would really start to holler about it and they would have to pull in their horns.

The response to this idea is in almost every case the same:

M6: Well, I think the check [under this plan] is the voter —

M4: Oh, but the *voter* —

M3: No, no — I respect the voter, but they can't get together on the problem the way the finance committee can.

In other circumstances the strategy suggested here might succeed. As a last resort, the agency seeking to control another agency may "throw them to the wolves" by suddenly assigning them responsibility for all aspects of a problem. The effectiveness of this maneuver depends, however, on the degree to which this expansion of function will in fact stimulate controls from other sources.

A related theme encountered in some of the discussions can be added to this list: the board of finance undertakes to insulate the board of education from external pressures, particularly "political" pressures. This protective function may in fact serve to free the other agency from distractions, but it may also effectively reduce its access to important power resources. The amorphous outlines of politics can be drawn to include the whole range of informal governmental negotiations as well as the cultivation of a friendly public. The agency seeking control can leave the other high and dry, vulnerable to the particular interpretations of politics the controller can impose—and all in the name of protecting the other's independence, non-partisanship, and discretion.

The purpose of these functional strategies can be simply summarized: it is to keep the other agency from "getting out of hand," without at the same time "tying their hands." Ambiguities in distinctions between policy and administration (level of generality), monetary and substantive decisions (medium of decision), and central and peripheral functions (scope of decision) make these strategies feasible.

INFORMATIONAL STRATEGIES

"I think it would be stupid not to have all the budgets go through one board—how could anything ever be figured out if you didn't have everything come through one channel?" This argument for a central position in the flow of information comes up repeatedly in the board of finance discussions and is related in a number of significant ways to the allocation of powers. Like the distribution of functions, the channeling of communications can be perceived as a technical problem, a matter of arranging the most efficient system for sharing relevant information. Much of the language used in discussing information flows is posed in just these terms. But around and beneath the technical considerations another set of meanings, involving the interplay of communication and power, is to be found. Insofar as knowledge is power, communications systems are power systems.[4]

The most obvious power move in this category is the demand for information from the agency to be controlled. Who has the right to ask questions of whom, to audit the books, to demand a report? Such questions come up continually:

[4]On the power implications of communications flows, see especially Karl W. Deutsch, *The Nerves of Government* (New York: Free Press of Glencoe, 1963), pt. II, especially ch. 11.

> M1: Do you think, for example, coming toward the end of the year, we could get a report from them as to how they're actually spending the monies that were appropriated?
>
> M2: You can request a report but they are under no obligation to give you a report.
>
> M1: Well, according to a gentleman's agreement, he promises to. I'm only bringing this into it because we would have some idea how close the budget is, and could see where he's padded and where he's short on another. Because towards the end of the year we always find that there's transfer of funds which would indicate that the budget's not a true one in the sense that they haven't asked for the requests in their proper place.
>
> M9: All their vouchers are still signed by Charley (the finance officer).
>
> M1: But we don't know—let's assume that he wants $50,000 for fuel and he gets by with forty. Now if he takes this other ten and uses it for something else would it be proper for us to know whether he did it or not?

As is evident in the case of legislative investigations generally, the demand for information can be a demand for compliance. If the investigator's preferences are known to the other agency and if the questions he asks are specific enough, the power implications can be very clear. In the budgetary process, further inquiries regarding an initial request are quite likely to be interpreted as pressure for reduction. As one chairman reports, "Occasionally the board has thrown something back to a selectman for more information, and once or twice the selectmen have found that they could do without it." Furthermore, the requirement of reports forces the other agency to state precisely matters which it might prefer to leave obscure; a detailed audit shows "where he's padded" and "stops people from figuring out a way to get rid of some money." The soft spots, the chinks in the armor are revealed. And especially if the information is communicated periodically, in written form, and through regular channels, it tends to commit the originator to a determined course of action. For all these reasons, the establishment of the right to know is an important power move.

On the other hand, the agency from which information is requested is by no means powerless to retaliate. One way is to insist on reciprocity; we'll share our secrets if you'll share yours. Another is to furnish so much information in such a complex and changing form—for instance, using special jargon or bizarre quantifications—that "they have us almost crazy trying to keep up with the thing." For example, a request for advice on the legal relationships between boards of finance and boards of education in Connecticut may bring forth so many conflicting and interlaced statutes regarding education—the board of education—what they shall, what they may, what cannot do. There's vagueness in my mind, without going back and studying each item, as to—are these a must as far as the state board rules are concerned, or are they not. Because you read one statute and it says in a town of a certain size the board of education *shall* do this and that, and then above or below that—with reference to education it says they *may* do so and so.

The best outcome from the school board's viewpoint may be the finance board's conclusion that, as one member says, "the board of education's business is so complicated that the board of finance couldn't possibly understand it and had no business to stick their noses into it anyway." Thus, the overloaded communications link burns out, and the school board is free to go its own way.

Another method for establishing control is infiltration, an intelligence operation for gathering information at first hand. This may begin with sending out observers to hearings or other public meetings, progress through the formal appointment of "liaison members" who sit in on the other agency's executive sessions, and end with the assumption of formal authority exercised through a voting representative. For example, one board of finance suggested a "controller," a "businessman" to keep track of financial matters within the school system. As the discussion develops, this proposed controller's powers steadily expand; he is conceived of as "handling the monies and purchases" for the board of education, then as "doing a businesslike job of managing their budget," and then as "directing the operation of that budget and seeing that it's maintained within the limits of it." Near the end of the discussion the controller is thought of as virtually taking over the school board for the board of finance.

> M8: Put in a finance director who'll be in charge of that budget.
> M3: It wouldn't be necessary for the board of finance to approve transfers if you had a controller.
> M5: He's an employee—remember you're hiring a man—you see, he would be answerable to some board like the board of finance; he would be an employee.

Only under exceptional circumstances could such a scheme be carried out in practice. A number of towns have, however, set up liaison systems by which individual board of finance members sit in on the deliberations of various requesting agencies. The countermove to this kind of infiltration is to seduce the infiltrator. As one liaison member to the board of selectmen explains:

You're sitting there with the selectmen, and you're getting the administration point of view, you're getting an overall picture of the entire town finances – and I think this detracts from your objective viewpoint on the merit of the particular program as presented to you. I think for that reason that some of the things about the budget that should be presented to the public are frequently not brought out in the hearing, because you've had the answer to it and the question we might raise at the public hearing has already been answered in the selectman's office.

As a lone interloper meeting time and again with the same committee, the representative from the board of finance finds it hard to keep his independent perspective.

These scattered examples illustrate some of the many ways in which information flows affect power relationships. Such strategies can be employed precisely because the distinction between information-seeking, in a neutral, technical, task-facilitative sense, and power-seeking is by no means clear.

TIMING

It is a mistake to think of a decision in government as something which occurs at a particular moment in time. Decision-making is a process, in which all but the most trivial decisions are developed over a series of stages extending from the first glimmer of an idea to the last time it is put into effect. The order and pace of the process have consequences for the distribution of power. Actors in the system make use of flexibilities in timing to advance their strategic purposes.[5]

A basic timing strategy is to get the other agency committed early in the game. For example, board of finance members continually complain that the school board, by contracting with teachers prior to submitting the annual education budget, in effect leaves the finance board no discretion.

> M2: Trouble with this is that they come to you with a *fait accompli* – the thing is done and there's no way –
> M1: That's right.
> M5: Yes.
> M1: Our hand is forced.
> M4: There's nothing we can do.

[5]On variations in time perspectives, see Robert E. Lane, *Political Ideology* (New York: Free Press of Glencoe, 1962), ch. 18. On commitment strategies, see Thomas C. Schelling, "An Essay on Bargaining," *American Economic Review*, LXVI (1956), 281-306; and Marvin E. Shaw, "A Serial Position Effect in Social Influence on Group Decisions," *Journal of Social Psychology*, LIV (1961), 83-91.

In some cases, they feel, "three-fourths or two-thirds of your budget is predetermined—of which you have absolutely no control" and "this is not evidence of good faith, and this is what makes me, for one, so damn mad sometimes that you feel you're shoveling whatchamacallit against the tide in general." Now, in fact, the board of finance could make things extremely difficult for the school board in this situation, perhaps by cutting its budget drastically until it conformed to the board of finance schedule. However, the result might be disastrous for the town: a reputation for broken commitments or long delays in making contracts could severely hamper teacher recruitment. What the board of education has done here is to *raise the stakes* of the game by getting its decisions fixed early in the budgetary sequence.

At the other end of this process a similar situation may arise. For example, in response to the argument that the board of finance really has very little power because the town meeting can, in the last analysis, override its decisions and the voters can refuse to reelect the members, one member says:

Well, the town meeting has the power of rejecting the budget or throwing the board of finance out. Now certainly no one wants to go that far—it isn't much of a shut-off. Sometimes they feel they should be in on the *making* of decisions, but they certainly don't want, just to get their own way, to throw the board of finance out, because the board of finance is doing a wonderful job. Neither do they want to throw the budget out because on the whole the budget is perfect, is good. To me, it's too far a swing.

Here the holding of "ultimate" power—the last say—fades into insignificance, insofar as the shaping of ordinary decisions is concerned. The possibility that radical sanctions could be imposed on the board of finance perhaps restrains it from departing too far from general community opinion (although the members' own political socialization plays the bigger role here), but the very radicalness of the ultimate sanctions argues strongly against their use. It appears, then, that one advantage of gaining an effective voice early in the decision process is that the farther along a decision has progressed the harder it is to change.

Another way to raise the cost of changing a decision late in the game is to interpret early commitments as binding in a moral sense, thus adding to the practical difficulties of late changes a difficulty of conscience. "To cut a budget," one member says, "means nothing unless the spirit of that cut is carried through"; another adds that once the two boards have "mutually agreed on a category, one party shouldn't have the ability to violate that agreement." At least two elements of flexibility make this a useful strategy: the early commitment may be considered a tentative or fixed one by one or both parties, and the implied terms of the agreement may be interpreted broadly or narrowly. For example, in referring back to previous budget decisions, the board of finance may argue that statements made in hearings by requesting officials were definite promises to be performed, while the requester may see them as highly tentative expressions of intention hedged with caveats about an uncertain future. One man's "contract" is another man's "educated guess."

Similarly, the inclusiveness of the early agreement is open to interpretation: did it encompass the detailed reasoning offered in support of a request or only the final figure arrived at? As one board of finance member argues,

Generally speaking, we have met with the board of education, they have come up with their decisions as to how they propose to spend the money for the coming school year. It has been heard by the public and the public has approved. And there is no reason why that board of education should deviate from their proposed plan.

The retrospective focus of these interpretations is evident: something done in an early stage is invested later with meaning not explicitly stated in the initial encounter.

Another timing strategy involves deciding whether to concentrate or disperse over time attention to particular decisions. For example, an agency may request gradual increases in nearly all items over the years, hoping that the moderateness of each increase will prevent drastic cutting. Or it may alternate requests for larger increases from one category to another, as this passage relates:

I do personally object to this freedom to do this because I think they can whipsaw you — they can whipsaw the taxpayer by transferring from a capital fund to a salary account. Then they get their salary account built up and they don't get the capital equipment that the townspeople voted for. So the next year they come back in for that capital equipment that they didn't get the prior year, plus maybe additional requests. And at the same time they get their salary schedule built up, so that they just whipsaw you right along the line.

The grounding for this strategy is the general assumption that a level of activity or expenditure will not be reduced significantly from that previously granted. A program acquires a "right" of sorts to the support accorded it in the last budget, plus a little bit more. But in order to expand and progress — that is, to increase its power — an agency must find ways to justify significantly higher levels of expenditure in at least some items. A one-thing-at-a-time approach — accompanied by arguments that, after all, no important increases in other programs are currently contemplated—may be effective for this purpose.

One last timing strategy deserves mention because it is frequently practiced, although probably more by inadvertance than by design. This is to delay a move until very shortly before a deadline so that others participating in the decision will not have time to consider it in detail. The advantage is surprise: the others lack "a chance to ask some preliminary questions and go back and think about it before you really hit that department." The risk is rejection of the entire plan, on the grounds that there is inadequate time to explore all its consequences and that "what is good today will be good tomorrow." As a one-shot, emergency device this strategy may work, but over the long run its credibility is very difficult to maintain.

FOUR FRAMES OF REFERENCE

Without much difficulty, this list of calculations and strategies could be much expanded. But since my aim is less to describe in detail what goes on in these particular committees than to suggest more general implications for understanding power operations, I turn to a discussion of what appear to be some basic frames of reference which shape the content of conversations about power.

We are dealing here with images of power, with communicated arguments and justifications—in a sense with the language of power—rather than with objectively measureable indicators of power. The two are not likely to be totally different, but it is clear that many of the links between argument and action are weak ones. The relevance of these images is that over the long run, and for most situations, they will provide a framework within which particular power decisions are in fact made.

As we saw for the board of finance discussions, four main contexts set conditions for power calculations and strategies. Now it is possible to see how these contexts relate to both limitations and potentialities of power strategies.

The historical context can be broadened to encompass all considerations of *time* in the processes of power. Time is a limiting factor: not everything can be done in the restricted amount of time available, so that selectivity is forced upon all participants. But there are variations, and in some respects the total time available is manipulable and its meaning varies with cultural differences in the meanings of time. For example, in the small, stable, closed village, it may take many years for a committee to build a favorable reputation for power, while the rapidly changing, frenetic, publicity-oriented big city may place a higher value on successful innovation and thus award favor on the basis of performance over a much briefer period. Time has its proprieties also in the short run. Tradition may impose restrictions on how fast decisions can be made. As Vidich and Bensman describe decision-making in one small community, the participants simply will not be rushed: the most trivial problems receive extended consideration. Where values of efficiency are dominant, moving rapidly has more positive connotations, and the prizes go to the committee which can "get things done."

These general time perspectives point toward the *relative* dimensions of amounts of time available. Within a particular community setting, some agencies have existed longer than others, some have more time in the month-to-month and day-to-day process than others do — time to learn, to plan, to negotiate. The significant variable in power relations among agencies may be not how long any one of them has been in operation, but which of them was there first. And it is often the difference between this committee and that committee in the time the short-run schedule allots to each which is important. Much as relative incomes can be more significant than absolute ones, relative allotments of time can set the conditions of power more determinatively than total amounts do.

Another way in which time is a power resource concerns sequences in the decision process. As we have seen, the agency which can make its voice heard in the early phases of a decision may have an advantage in some situations. The ability to get others committed from the first to some general or partial definition of the problem, to reiterate and reinterpret this commitment as deliberations proceed, and thus to build up the cost of altering this position — these are probably some of the strongest power strategies in use. In other situations — particularly where continuous supervision is difficult — participation in later, executory phases may be determinative. Or an agency may be able to reverse certain sequences or stretch out its participation (e.g., by infiltrating earlier or later phases) over a longer temporal segment of the process.

Thus he who can decide

(*a*) how long a particular process can take,

(*b*) how fast each stage in this process must be traversed, and

(*c*) in what order the participation of the agencies will take place, has the makings of a strong position in the structuring of power.

The second major context for decisions, the technical context, can be generalized to a more inclusive *cognitive* dimension. Every decision is potentially extremely complex: the number of possibly relevant facts is immense, few of them are readily available, and none of them speak for themselves. At the outside, the inability of the human brain to accommodate more than a tiny part of the information presented to it sets limits to the power of knowledge. Devices for simplifying reality are essential for action. Such techniques as focusing on the immediate past and future and on the spatially close at hand are familiar. These techniques are at once too easy, since they are available to any actor in the system, and too hard, since they are never fully effective and involve costs and risks which can seldom be included in the calculations.

From a power perspective, cognitive considerations can be manipulated in a number of significant ways. The most obvious is secrecy versus access — who has the right to know what? A committee may go to great lengths to protect its "private" information, particularly information about internal conflicts, perhaps by establishing and broadening the scope of executive or informal deliberations. The strategic problem here is to gain consent for a classification system — covering either certain places or categories of documents or both — which defines key information as the rightful property of the agency, to be shared only through the discretion of the owner.

But in a democracy secrecy will always be a relatively weak strategy, as difficult to justify as to execute. In the last analysis, the public has a right to know and the press is there to claim it for them. A far more effective set of cognitive strategies involves manipulating the *attention* of participants toward some aspects of the situation and away from others. Information which cannot be hidden can be obscured or highlighted in several ways, all of which take advantage of the fact that not everything seen is perceived, that cognitive maps are never flat but are mountains and valleys, light and shadow.

As in the case of some budgeting moves, attention can be diverted by increasing the cost of paying attention. The significant facts can be buried in a mass of irrelevancy, posed in highly technical or vague language, or in such a way as to require complex analysis before the point is clear. Yet the demand for information has been met. Other items can be emphasized by all the usual arts of propaganda, by verbal emphasis, interest-arousing language, repetition, and so on.

More basic methods for manipulating attention involve shaping the general approach to a topic and the rules of evidence to apply in considering it. The way the over-all problem is defined establishes in a relatively abstract and inclusive way criteria of relevance which tend to guide all deliberations on particulars. The problem may be posed at a high or low level of generality, thus directing attention to broad principles or to one detail after another. It may be defined as a matter for negotiated compromise, a winner-take-all outcome, or a decision on the merits of each subquestion. And the substance of the problem can be set so as to shape the answers – for example, "Where are we going to build this school?" versus "Should we build a school?"

In the discussions we have reviewed, specific rules of evidence are seldom clearly stated and agreed upon. More often they are invoked and altered to suit particular arguments. Yet their cumulative impact on outcomes can hardly be exaggerated. The committee which habitually decides by cursory, informal, spur-of-the-moment recounting of anecdotes and opinions thus allows a freer play for the members' personal predispositions and, more significantly, for shared attitudes. In such cases evidence will be selected and emphasized to shape decisions in accord with the committee's initial norms and orientations. From a power perspective, the strategy to pursue is to work on these attitudes rather than on the systematic development of information. On the other hand, deliberations beginning with an orderly, step-by-step review of available information, selected on the basis of some fixed criteria, are more constrained. Manipulation of shared attitudes is less effective; the power problem becomes one of affecting the rules of evidence themselves.

As has been shown, there are numerous possibilities. Long- or short-run averages or trends can be invoked; critical or hypothetical cases can be stressed. Comparisons can be restricted to those within certain categories or extended to a broader frame of reference in time or space. The particular outcomes implicit in these criteria will vary from situation to situation, but it is clear that the special ways evidence is handled can be an important stake in the search for power.

The context of shared powers – the functional division of labor – can be broadened for analytical purposes to include all references to control of the *organizational means* for accomplishing valued ends. The basic outline of organizational means, the pluralistic bargaining system, is a given; participants rarely propose in any explicit way the imposition of hierarchy. But within this framework there is much room for maneuvering. The science of administration has yet to produce definitive recommendations for the best practical functional relationships, and, in any case, few participants are aware of such recommendations as have been made. Arguments are available to support a multitude of contradictory functional arrangements.

Preceding the problem of defining functional relationships is the question of whether or not, or how precisely, they are to be defined. The advocate of "clear lines of authority and responsibility" can be resisted on grounds that the present system, while organizationally sloppy, "works," and that in a rapidly changing environment organizational responsibilities should not be frozen into a rigid mold. The point here is that these ploys are never neutral as regards the distribution of power. Typically the champions of jurisdictional clarity seem to be those who think or feel that they have a valid claim to increased authority, one likely to receive support from wider audiences, and that a sharper set of definitions will produce a favorable redistribution of authority or at least protection for the power they presently exercise.

Once the argument that functional relationships should be defined is accepted, power strategies are facilitated by several ambiguities concerning the proper definition. The appropriateness of control at a particular level of generality, through a certain medium, over an inclusive or restricted scope of decision—all these are arguable matters. In order to lay claim to a jurisdiction held by another agency, one must pry it loose from that cluster of functions and cement it to one's own cluster. The process involves, in the first place, calling attention to discontinuities in the other's collection of functions, usually by emphasizing the distinctiveness of the central, essential functions the other performs. Why should an agency whose whole effort should be bent toward the education of the young have the distracting duty of cutting the schoolyard grass? Or why should it be bothered with matters of general policy, or with the technical complexities of bookkeeping? These arguments emphasize weak links in the chain of functions which the other agency performs. The standard defense against this tactic is to stress the interdependencies among all the agency's functions. Emphasis is placed on the agency's total package of functions and on the complexity of relationships among these functions. For example, the board of education should control grass-cutting because it must protect the children from dangerous machinery, prevent noisy disruptions of classroom teaching, keep questionable characters away from school grounds, determine the use of its own storage space, and so on. Any particular function is seen as inextricably imbedded in an interlocking network of activities essential to the performance of the agency's major distinctive function.

Perhaps this point can be posed more generally: the agency seeking control tends to proceed by *abstract* analysis, by concentrating on distinctions among activities on the basis of their defining properties. The defending agency tends to proceed *empirically*, by demonstrating how in actual situations its various functions blend and merge. The arguments never quite meet. But whichever party can push the question over into its preferred frame of reference has a power advantage.

The power-seeking agency's second problem is simpler: to attach the desired function to its own collection of activities. Attention is focused on similarities between the function sought and the agency's normal ones. If the power-seeking agency has been performing similar functions for a longer time, on a larger scale, and more efficiently, the argument for taking over the new function is strengthened. The argument will almost always be a combination of appeals to a proprietary "right" to the job, based on earlier entry or predominant concern, and to the general criterion of operational efficiency.

In a sense the *moral dimension* of power incorporates all of the above. That is, the primary ethical rule is that some plausible justification be offered for any power move. This is due, in the main, to cultural norms imbedded in the consciences of the participants, norms which condemn "dictatorship," "domination," "authoritarianism," and "compulsion," and which value "independence," "equality," "consideration," and "persuasion." But it probably also reflects a situational element: the more pluralistic and public the system, the more pressure to rationalize power moves, to consider the problem of persuasion as an essential part of the decision process. In most cases, explanations of some sort cannot be avoided. But a variety of ambiguities in the moral context allow for strategic selection.

Beyond the obvious looseness of fit between any broad ethical generalization and any application to particular circumstances, at least two other dimensions permit flexibility. First, although assumptions about the moral character of the participants are seldom examined in any thorough, explicit way, they are continually invoked to back up this or that strategic move. Regarding either mankind in general or a specific other group, character evaluations appear to concern both (*a*) goodness or badness of *will* and (*b*) reliability or unreliability in *the exercise of will*. It is easy to see that one's arguments for control can be justified if the other is perceived as reliably bad, good but unsteady, or both bad and unreliable. In practice, however, the other is only very rarely characterized as evil in any fundamental way. Rather the following three arguments are the ones most often encountered:

1. All men, including the other agency, are primarily motivated by self-interest. Pursuit of self-interest is legitimate and expected. Therefore only a system of checks and balances can protect against bad outcomes.
2. The others mean well, but their vision is too narrow. They fail to take into account the broader, longer-range interests of the society, and therefore need the corrective influence of those who can do so.
3. The others mean well, but their incompetence and/or susceptibility to external pressures renders them unreliable. Their

intentions are irrelevant because they are unable to adhere to them steadily. Like children, they need the guidance of steadier hands.

A second moral dimension of power concerns defining the ends for which a particular power process exists. Empirically there are few references to ideology, in the sense of a full-blown conception of the good society. But there is continual resort to intermediate goals – those more inclusive than day-to-day survival and less inclusive than the general welfare. The strategic importance of these intermediate goals lies in their organizing influence, since the way they are defined determines what activities are considered instrumental to what other activities. Ambiguities arise because the end purpose of the process can be perceived in many different ways. The key strategic move appears to be: get the goal defined as the activity under your control. For example, the budget discussions between the board of finance and the board of education could proceed on the assumption that the end product is either (*a*) the over-all, completed town budget or (*b*) class-room education. Emphasis on the budget as a goal (or, more precisely, on a balanced or low-cost or "reasonable" budget) relegates educational goals to a subsidiary status, makes them significant only insofar as they affect the general level of revenues and expenditures. Hence, the hand of the board of finance is strengthened. Emphasis on education in the classroom places budgeting in an instrumental category, subject to criteria of rationality and efficiency in relation to educational goals, and, thus, strengthens the board of education. He who can say, "The whole process culminates here," and be believed, has an important power resource.

The exercise of power, in summary, is both limited and made possible by certain images of power which the participants share. In particular, arguments about power are posed within a framework of relevant but ambiguous concepts – time, knowledge, organization, and values. Questions the participants consider important can be raised along any or all of these dimensions because there are no "correct," authoritative answers available to them. The particular answers they agree on have significant implications for the distribution of power; viewed from a different perspective, these answers are strategies for gaining and holding power.

Yet the words people use to describe their activities are suspect data. In the absence of other evidence, we listen to the ways they talk and try to interpret what they mean. Before proceeding to examine some more nearly objective elements of power, it may be useful to illustrate briefly, in the next chapter, how images of power are shaped by the mind of the beholder.

CHAPTER IV

Cognitive Dissonance and the Perception of Power

IN THE PRECEDING chapter, I tried to illustrate how political power is a *cultural* phenomenon: power is shaped and distributed and concentrated by participants in accordance with certain shared values and perceptions. The method was inductive: combing through the transcripts of the discussions, we see what common themes are invoked as each group goes about making detailed decisions. The advantage of this method, I would argue, is that it gets at values and perceptions which are operative, in that they are linked by the respondents themselves to the practical problems and solutions which they develop. These themes provide a rough but workable philosophy and epistemology of power.

There are, however, those who would object to the indirection of this method. If one wants to know how these leaders view power in their communities, why not ask them? Why try to guess what they mean from what they say as they work? This chapter is an attempt to show some of the pitfalls involved in a more direct approach. As it turns out, responses to a direct inquiry about community power may not be helpful as indicators of political reality—but they do provide some interesting insights into political beliefs.

DISSENSUS ON COMMUNITY POWER STRUCTURE

In the questionnaires administered immediately after the discussion on the board of education problem, each member was asked to choose "which of the following two statements comes closer to describing decision-making in the town" (Q 29). The alternative statements were:

A

Almost all important community decisions are made by a small group of people. These few leaders usually take the initiative in starting projects; they almost always stop any project they oppose. Members of this group frequently get together informally to discuss their plans. Their influence is dominant over nearly all community affairs, regardless of the subject. They seldom find it necessary to concern themselves much with the opinions of other groups or individuals. In short, the town is pretty much run by a small group of persons with a great deal of influence.

B

Almost all important community decisions are made by a process of give and take among a large number of groups and individuals. On one issue, one combination of interested people will develop; on another issue, an almost entirely different combination is formed. Many different persons bring up important issues for consideration; there is no one group which can stop nearly every project. Leaders find it necessary to pay close attention to what most people are thinking in the community. In short, the town is pretty much run by constantly changing alliances in which many individuals and groups play significant parts.

Six answer categories allowed the respondent to indicate whether he saw the town as "much more," "somewhat more," or "slightly more" like one or the other alternative. The shades of preference were subsequently combined to distinguish simply between those who chose A, the elitist alternative, and those who chose B, the pluralist alternative. All but one of the 85 members answered this question.

Table IV.1 shows the distribution of responses for each of the twelve boards. The first thing we notice is that there is considerable disagreement among members of the same board regarding the general outlines of power in the community. In only one board, Board 9, are the members unanimous in their choice. Nor is there any clear trend in either the elitist or the pluralist direction as we move from the small to the larger towns. Each of the small towns divides on the question as closely as possible. In the middle towns, one is split, two lean in the elitist direction, and one leans toward pluralism. Two of the larger towns have majorities for the elitist view and two for the pluralist view.

The picture is not particularly clarified when we look only at the seven boards which deviate from the closest possible split (Boards 6 through 12). For example, we might expect that towns characterized as elitist would display a lower level of political conflict than those viewed as pluralist. But statistics on political conflict show no consistent pattern: competition between the two political parties was just about as close in the elitist towns as in the pluralist towns. The four elitist towns were 64, 39, 51, and 54 per cent Republican in party registration

TABLE IV.1
Perceived Power Structure and Community Population

Population Category	Elitist	Pluralist
Small Towns (1,200 to 2,900)		
Board 1	3	4
Board 2	3	3
Board 3	3	3
Board 4	3	4
Middle Towns (7,300 to 19,500)		
Board 5	2	2
Board 6	6	3
Board 7	5	2
Board 8	2	6
Larger Towns (30,000 to 46,200)		
Board 9	8	0
Board 10	6	3
Board 11	1	3
Board 12	3	6
Total	45	39

in 1960; the three pluralist towns had Republican registrations of 57, 67, and 25 per cent. The average winning margins in percentage of votes for the local chief executive in the three most recent elections were 4, 21, and 3 percentage points for the pluralist towns and 2, 12, 1, and 13 percentage points for the elitist towns. Perhaps other data would show a more definite pattern, but at least in terms of partisan divisions there is no clear difference between towns which the board members tend to see as dominated by a power elite and those seen as pluralistic.

In the last chapter we have seen how, in the course of making practical decisions, members of the boards of finance tend to accept a pluralistic view of power in their communities. They refer again and again to the necessity for bargaining, the desirability of cooperation among equals. We infer from this that there is a shared, positive orientation toward pluralism which tends to shape actual decisions on specific policy proposals. But when the question is posed at a higher level of abstraction, as in the paragraphs above, the members show much more mixed preferences. The reason for this apparent contradiction probably lies in disparities between highly generalized opinions and opinions invoked in particular contexts.[1] A person may adhere to a

[1]There is much evidence for this in political opinion studies. See, for example, James W. Prothro and Charles M. Grigg, "Fundamental Principles of Democracy: Bases of Agreement and Disagreement," *Journal of Politics*, XXII (1960), 276-94; and Samuel H. Stouffer, *Communism, Conformity, and Civil Liberties* (Garden City, N.Y.: Doubleday, 1955).

general belief in freedom of speech—and yet bring other values to bear when he is considering whether or not to allow an atheist to teach in the public schools. In much the same way a public official embroiled in a highly pluralistic situation, and continually invoking pluralistic premises as he makes day-to-day decisions, may nevertheless agree, when asked, that a small coterie of influentials runs his town. As evidence in specifying the objective realities of decision-making, broad generalizations by participants are obviously suspect.

As need-fulfilling opportunities, however, such generalizations are of interest. The links between very abstract beliefs and practical action are weak; this means that, to a large degree, a person can believe what he wants or needs to without this interfering much with his behavior. Viewed from this perspective, the choice between alternative models of community decision-making as posed in the elitist-pluralist question probably indicates more about the person answering than about the realities of power in his community. Some of our data illustrate how it is that the kind of general report on power in his community that a board of finance member might convey to the researcher can represent personal needs more than political realities.

PERCEPTIONS OF SELF AND PERCEPTIONS OF POWER

The data concern relationships between self-images and images of community power.[2] The hypothesis is that a person will tend to perceive a community power structure which is consistent with his perception of himself. Or, to put it the other way around, he will tend to choose that description of community power which is less dissonant with his self-image than other descriptions are. The self-image is a fundamental feature of personality; the image of community power is a derivative, relatively peripheral perception, one with only tenuous behavioral implications. Consequently, the person is relatively constrained in altering his self-image, but relatively free to shape his image of power. Before attempting a more thorough explanation, let us see how some responses by the board of finance members fit this interpretation.

A primary dimension of a person's self-image is evaluation—one perceives himself as doing relatively well or relatively poorly in impor-

[2]On relationships between self-images and perceptions, see David Krech, Richard S. Crutchfield, and Egerton L. Ballachey, *Individual in Society* (New York: McGraw-Hill, 1962), ch. 3. On vagaries involved in reports of community power, see Raymond E. Wolfinger, "Reputation and Reality in the Study of 'Community Power,'" *American Sociological Review*, XXV (1960), 636-44; and Nelson W. Polsby, *Community Power and Political Theory* (New Haven, Conn.: Yale University Press, 1963), pp. 47ff.

tant activities. Two items in the questionnaires provide evidence on self-evaluation. Members were asked, "How would you rate your own performance so far on the board of finance?" (Q 13) Answer categories were Superior, Excellent, Fair, Poor, and Very Poor. No one selected the last of these ratings, so the responses could logically be divided between high (superior or excellent) and low (fair or poor) self-evaluations.

Another question, placed elsewhere in the questionnaire, asked the respondent to complete the sentence, "When I am a leader I am usually . . . ," with Excellent, Very good, Fair, or Not so good (F5C). Again the first two answers were scored as high and the second two as low.

In Tables IV.2 and IV.3, the relationship between these self-evaluations and images of community power is indicated. The data suggest that there is some tendency for those who rate themselves high as members and as leaders to see the community as elitist; those who are more critical of their own performance tend to perceive a pluralist power structure.

TABLE IV.2
Perceived Power Structure and Self-Rating of Performance
as a Board of Finance Member

Self-Rating of Performance	Elitist	Pluralist	Total	N
High	68%	32%	100%	28
Low	41	59	100	46

TABLE IV.3
Perceived Power Structure and Evaluation of Self as Leader

Self-Evaluation	Elitist	Pluralist	Total	N
High	59%	41%	100%	49
Low	44	56	100	34

A second dimension of the self-image concerns dominance. A person may see himself as one who typically plays a directive, authoritative role with others, or he may stress mutuality and cooperation in his interpersonal relationships. A question from William Schutz's FIRO-B series provided data on these tendencies (F 2). The respondents were asked to choose between the following descriptions of their own behavior, one (on the right) emphasizing directiveness, and the other (on the left) emphasizing sharing:

When I am responsible for organizing and carrying out a task, the most important thing to me is to try to include those who are working with me in the decisions and the responsibility I have. I consult them before I make a decision, and we discuss it and try to come to agreement about what should be done. After the discussion I try to divide up the task and have everyone take responsibility for his own part. Then if anyone fails to do what he should, it's up to him to correct it. When someone does fail to do his job I usually don't exert my authority but let the group work it out themselves.

When I am responsible for organizing and carrying out a task, the most important things I try to do are make sure everyone knows exactly what is expected of him and make sure I know my job thoroughly. Then I try to see to it that the task is carried out according to the rule laid down. If I let anyone violate the rules we're following without being disciplined, I lose the respect of those under me, my authority and effectiveness are endangered, and it is not fair to those who are doing their job. Sometimes it is necessary to make an example of someone by disciplining him publically so that the others know the rules are being enforced.

Table IV.4 shows the distribution of responses to this question and to the elitist-pluralist descriptions of community power. It appears that individuals who see themselves as playing a rather directive role are more likely to see their communities as elitist, while those who stress mutuality and cooperation in their interpersonal relationships are prone to see these qualities in their community too. The tendencies toward congruence between one's self-image and his perception of community power are evident.

TABLE IV.4
Perceived Power Structure and Self-Rating of Directiveness as Leader

Self-Rating of Directiveness	Elitist	Pluralist	Total	N
High	67%	33%	100%	30
Low	45	55	100	53

A third dimension of the self-image is affectional, the degree to which a person sees himself as engaged in warm, close relationships with others or as more withdrawn and impersonal. Another question from Schutz's FIRO-B series (F 1) taps this aspect of the self-image. The alternative statements were:

I try to keep my relations with people on a fairly impersonal basis. I really don't enjoy getting too involved with people, partly because it interferes with my desire to be by myself. I don't especially appreciate people coming to visit me at any hour, though I do recognize they're just trying to be friendly. There are many times I don't feel like seeing people — I'm content with what I'm doing. I feel that I can handle my personal problems better by myself. If I want to talk about them with anyone I would rather it be someone I don't know well than a close friend. In a group I don't get involved with personalities but prefer to stick to what we're supposed to be doing.

I try to make friends as quickly as possible with virtually everyone I meet. To me, being liked is the most important thing. I try to have my relationships with people informal and very close. I like to discuss personal problems with close friends. I like people to drop in on me at almost any hour of the day or night, and practically always I will go out somewhere with them if they ask me to. I will go out of my way to make people like me and do a great deal to avoid being disliked by them. Sharing experiences and being partly responsible to others is very important. In a group I almost always try to get to know the other members well, because I enjoy the group more then.

Table IV.5 shows the distribution of responses on the dimension of personalism. Those who choose the alternative stressing warm, close relationships with others are also likely to see their community as dominated by an elite. The socially cooler members tend to see a more pluralistic power structure.

One additional set of answers shows how elitists and pluralists tend to differ in the needs they seek to satisfy through participation in

TABLE IV.5

Perceived Power Structure and Self-Rating of Personalism in Social Relations

Self-Rating of Personalism	Elitist	Pluralist	Total	N
High	61%	39%	100%	44
Low	42	58	100	38

group activities. Members were asked to complete the sentence, "When I am in a group, the thing I like most is to be . . .," by ranking three possibilities: Very well liked, A leader, and Prominent in the activities (F5D). In Table IV.6 these responses are scored high (first or second choice) or low (third choice) and related to the perceived power structure. The results show a slight tendency for those who value being liked and leading to select the elitist description, while those who want to be prominent in the activities of the group are far more apt to choose the pluralist one.

TABLE IV.6

**Perceived Power Structure and Self-Estimation of Desired Rewards
from Participation in Group Activities**

Self-Estimation of Desired Rewards	Elitist	Pluralist	Total	N
Being Liked				
High (first or second choice)	56%	44%	100%	50
Low (third choice)	36	64	100	28
Being a Leader				
High	55	45	100	40
Low	41	59	100	34
Being Prominent				
High	44	56	100	68
Low	92	8	100	13

These marginal tendencies can be summarized as follows. Elitists — those who perceive their communities as dominated by a power elite — are more likely to be those who perceive themselves as excellent performers as members and leaders, exercising dominance when in a leadership role, and striving for close, affectional relationships with others. Pluralists — those who see their communities as run by bargaining among a wide variety of power centers — are more likely to be those who perceive themselves as performing less capably as members or leaders, using a cooperative leadership style, and seeking independence and individual prominence in their social relationships.

How are these findings to be explained? It seems evident that the broad and simple characterizations of community power offered in the elitist-pluralist alternatives have little direct connection with the kinds of operative assumptions upon which the members base their actions. It is probably true that public officials, like other people, seldom act on the basis of deduction from general principles; that is, the usual mode of decision-making does not proceed from the abstract to the concrete, but the other way around.[3] Typically the decision-maker finds himself confronted with a practical situation involving choice. Most of his attention is taken up with the factual details of this situation. But in part to guide his decision and in part to justify his intuitive preference, he refers to a collection of generalities, rarely formulated in any systematic way, and selects certain of them as relevant to the particular choice he has to make. These moral and behavioral premises are invoked to fit a special set of circumstances and are expressed when and if they appear to have persuasive possibilities in the group deliberations. The resulting collection of expressed (shared) premises consti-

[3]Cf. Jerome S. Bruner *et al.*, *A Study of Thinking* (New York: Wiley, 1956).

tutes the operative political culture of the group. If these common premises depart very far from reality the group will fail in its attempts to adapt to the environment in which it operates. The penalties for groups and for individual members of groups who do not adhere to realistic principles in their everyday operations can be severe.

But there are few penalties for idiosyncratic beliefs held by individuals so long as these are not invoked or expressed in some context of action. As isolated items in a person's storehouse of generalities, they are available for other purposes, for meeting needs other than the need for rationalizing decisions.

The self-image, on the other hand, is a central feature of personality. Although dependent to some extent on immediate external circumstances, and subject to some change over time, the self-image tends toward stability and persistence. Consequently, when there is a conflict between one's image of himself and some highly abstract perceptual formulation regarding the world around him, it is the latter which is likely to be distorted to fit the former. In the case of our elitist-pluralist dichotomy, this explanation appears to fit the evidence.

Clearly members of a board of finance are in a position to think of themselves as part of any power elite in their town. As formulated in the questionnaire, the elitist alternative stresses at least three features of the elite: exclusiveness, directiveness, and cohesiveness. Each of these features tends to resonate with an element of the self-image. The exclusive aspect is emphasized in the characterization of the elite as a "small group," a "few leaders," who "seldom find it necessary to concern themselves with the opinions of other groups or individuals." A boundary is drawn, a distinction perceived, between the select few and the excluded many. This distinction is much more blurred in the pluralist alternative, in which "a large number of groups and individuals," "many different persons," "constantly changing alliances," are described as involved in important decisions. Here the consonance between the elitist viewpoint and a high self-evaluation is clear. The person who thinks he is an excellent performer has a psychological stake in a view of the community which stresses the distinctiveness of the ruling group. Such a perception supports and enhances his sense of being a bit better, a cut above the others in terms of ability and effectiveness. An equalitarian community, on the other hand, renders less relevant the possession of higher talents. Free to select an elitist or a pluralist general description of community power — because the choice need not make much difference in practice — the man who thinks of himself as exceptional is apt to find the elitist view the more comfortable one. Pluralists tend to be more self-critical (although not necessarily self-denigrating) and, thus, to feel more at home with a community power description which puts less emphasis on distinctions in personal qualifications.

The elitist alternative also stresses directiveness: the elite is "dominant over nearly all community affairs," and "the town is pretty much run by a small group of persons with a great deal of influence," who "almost always stop any project they oppose." Leadership, as described in the pluralist alternative, is much more cooperative: there is a "process of give and take," initiative and veto power are widespread, and leaders cannot afford to neglect public opinion. The self-perception, "I am dominant," is obviously more consonant with the elitist characterization than with the pluralist one. The person who sees himself as directive, authoritative, and disciplinary feels at home in a system organized for the exercise of direction, authority, and discipline. Similarly one who conceives of himself as a negotiator finds his place more readily in a pluralistic system. In both cases, the temptation is to warp perceptions in these need-fulfilling ways.

Finally, the elitist position stresses the cohesiveness, the intimacy, of relationships among the elite. They form an in-group; they "frequently get together informally to discuss their plans." The person who values warm relationships with others, who wants to be liked even more than he wants to lead or take a prominent part, tends to be attracted by this aspect of elitism. The more distant individualist, or the man who actively resists social intimacy, feels more comfortable in a less cozy political environment, one in which the commitment to others is looser and more tentative. Again, the psychologically peripheral perception of community power tends to be altered to fit the psychologically central self-image.

These pieces of evidence suggest tendencies rather than laws, marginal shadings rather than blacks and whites. But they are, perhaps, distinct enough to indicate the necessity, in the investigation of political power cultures, to ask the right questions about the right data. If the purpose is to understand linkages between images and actions, the analysis calls for concentration on the ways in which these elements are connected in practice.[4] To suppose that adherence to some general position implies some particular set of choices about specific

[4]See Richard D. Mann, "A Review of the Relationships between Personality and Performance in Small Groups," *Psychological Bulletin,* LVI (1959), 241-70; and A. Paul Hare, *Handbook of Small Group Research* (New York: Free Press of Glencoe, 1962), ch. 6.

policies is to suggest a hypothesis rather than to announce an obvious truth. Conversely, it is dangerous to leap from data about the premises invoked in the course of decision-making to predictions about the participant's reactions to abstract statements. As Justice Holmes put it, "General propositions do not decide concrete cases." Nor did the concrete cases necessarily determine the general propositions, in the minds of our respondents.

With these precautions in mind, I turn next to some empirical connections between one image of power—formal authority—and the behaviors which it engenders.

CHAPTER V

Formal Leadership: The Chairman

LIKE MANY OTHER small committees in government, the boards of finance have only one explicitly formalized position of leadership: the chairman. Unlike the situation in many experimental small groups, there is no ambiguity in identifying the formal leader. He knows who he is; the others know who he is. The position and its accompanying higher status are clear.

But what is the chairman of a committee supposed to do? Identifying the position helps little in defining the role. No manual specifies his style of action. In fact there are several problematical ambiguities facing the man who takes on the chairman's job. For instance, is he responsible for initiating practical suggestions for solving the group's problems, for leadership in the sense of making proposals? Or should he confine himself to strictly procedural guidance? Should he take sides in a controversy or remain neutral among the contenders? Is it his job to control the group process by insisting that definite procedures be adhered to? Or should he usually let the group go its own way, stepping in only in cases of complete confusion? These questions have a common element—the general distinction between activity and passivity, between the initiating-contending-controlling chairman and the moderating-neutral-permissive one. If we recognize that many nuances will be lost in the process, we can categorize the twelve chairmen of our laboratory groups into the more active and the less active, for purposes of comparison. We shall attempt to determine how the more active chairmen differ from the less active ones in the resources and attitudes they bring to the board deliberations, in their styles of action as chairmen, and in the types of responses these styles elicit from the other members.

For this purpose, each chairman is assigned an activity score which is the ratio of his total number of initiations (i.e., all acts so scored by Bales Interaction Process Analysis) to the average number of initiations for members of his group. Active chairmen are those ranking first through sixth on this ratio (range 2.3 to 1.6); passive chairmen are those ranking seventh through twelfth (range 1.4 to .8).

In comparing these two categories, we shall look particularly for differences which are (*a*) large enough to suggest significance, and (*b*) fairly consistent across the full slate of twelve chairmen. Thus we shall not only contrast active and passive chairmen as categories, but also show the number of comparisons between individual active and passive chairmen that are consistent with the direction of the contrast between the two categories. For example, if on any measure *each* of the six more active chairmen scores higher than *any* of the six less active chairmen, then the relationship holds for 36 of the 36 possible comparisons for that measure; if one passive chairman has a higher score than one active chairman, the relationship holds for 35 of the 36 comparisons, and so forth.

RESOURCES AND ATTITUDES

Why are some chairmen active and others passive? A first clue emerges when we look at the differences in the resources which chairmen bring to their board of finance work and their attitudes toward participation in that work. We need to know what makes a man *able* to engage in active leadership—the particular skills and statuses he draws upon—and what makes him *desire* to exercise leadership. On both scores the active and passive chairmen differ markedly.

In the first place, as Table V.1 shows clearly, the two categories draw on different types of resources. The active chairman has a considerably stronger educational background and has achieved a much higher level of income. His experience in attending conferences in his regular occupation makes it easier for him to speak out in the board of finance meeting. The passive chairman, on the other hand, is older and has a longer history in the town. Both, however, have about the same seniority on the board itself.

Comparing individual chairmen on these dimensions might obscure group characteristics which account for the contrasts. For instance, we might suspect that all members of small town boards, including the chairmen, would be less active, less educated, less

TABLE V.1

Contrasting Resources of Active and Passive Chairmen

Resource	Mean for Active Chairmen	Mean for Passive Chairmen	Number of Comparisons in which Difference Is as Expected
Income (Q60)	$18,200	$8,080	35 out of 36
Education (Q58)	15.7 yrs.	12.2 yrs.	24 out of 36
Frequency of conferences in occupation (Q50) (range 4-7)	6.4	4.6	20 out of 25*
Seniority (Q6)	4.5 yrs.	4.8 yrs.	12 out of 36
Age (Q53)	54.8 yrs.	60.2 yrs.	25 out of 36
Years in town (Q51)	27.0	40.8	28 out of 36

*Question was not answered by two chairmen.

affluent, and older. This is not the case. In fact, the active and passive categories each includes two chairmen from each of the three population categories: small towns, ranging from 1,200 to 2,900, middle-sized towns, from 7,300 to 19,500, and large towns, from 30,000 to 46,200. To check on other possible group effects, we can see whether or not the findings in Table V.1 hold when the chairman's resources are considered in relation to those of the average member of his group.

Table V.2 summarizes comparisons between active and passive chairmen on five group-related measures. Each is calculated by averaging the ratios between each chairman's score and the mean for his group. In addition to age, years in town, and seniority, two composite

TABLE V.2

Resources of Active and Passive Chairmen in Relation to Their Group Averages (Group Average = 1.0)

	Mean for Active Chairmen	Mean for Passive Chairmen	Number of Comparisons which Differ as the Means Do
Socioeconomic status	1.6	.6	31 out of 36
Social intercourse	1.0	.7	21 out of 36
Seniority	1.1	1.0	19 out of 36
Age	1.1	1.2	25 out of 36
Years in town	.9	1.3	27 out of 36

indices are compared: socioeconomic status and social intercourse. The first of these indices is composed by summing the chairman's scores on four dichotomized (0,1) variables: income, education, occupational status, and self-identified social class. The social intercourse index is the sum of scores on dichotomized responses to questions on frequency of attending conferences as a part of one's work, occupational time spent talking, and frequency of social visiting outside the home.

When the scores for chairmen are calculated in relation to their group averages, differences between active and passive chairmen in age and seniority practically disappear. That is, the quiet chairman is no more likely to stand out in his group as one of the older or more senior members than the talkative chairman is. But active chairmen maintain a marked and consistent advantage in socioeconomic status,[1] and, to a lesser degree, in frequency of social intercourse. In fact, the passive chairman is apt to have less status and to participate less in social intercourse than the average member of his group. On the other hand, passive chairmen stand out to some extent as long-time residents of their towns, compared with others in their groups, while the active ones are about like their fellow members in this respect.

Thus, part of the explanation for the higher participation rates of active chairmen is that they have the verbal ability and confidence which high education, conversational experience, and occupational achievement engender. These qualities overcome their relative lack of long experience with local matters.

In addition, there is at least some evidence that the active chairmen are more likely to see themselves as operating within a *political* context, one requiring the energetic pursuit of compromise. Four of the six active chairmen reported that their parents "were interested in politics and government" (Q56), compared to only two of the six passive chairmen. Four of the active chairmen had held elective office prior to becoming board of finance members (Q8), compared to one of the passive chairmen. In choosing between alternative descriptions of the power structure in their towns (Q29), four of the active chairmen chose the pluralist description, stressing the "give and take . . . among constantly changing alliances in which many individuals and groups play significant parts"; while the passive chairmen opted four to two for an elitist alternative: "almost all important community decisions are made by a small group of people. . . ." In choosing among four descriptions of town goals[2] "which you tend to stress most as impor-

---

[1]For a finding that among adults in mock jury deliberations, leadership is strongly associated with socioeconomic status, see F. L. Strodtbeck, Rita M. James, and C. Hawkins, "Social Status in Jury Deliberations," *American Sociological Review,* XXII (1957), 713-19.

[2]Descriptions of town goals (Q29a) were suggested by an article by Oliver P. Williams, "A Typology for Comparative Local Government," *Midwest Journal of Political Science,* V (1961), 150-64. I am grateful to Professor Williams for commenting on my formulations.

tant" (Q29a), four of the active and only one of the passive chairmen chose the following paragraph:

The main goal of our town government should be to make compromises of issues as they arise. The views of different groups should be taken into account, and a workable balance reached. The government represents the people; town officials should make themselves available for any citizens or groups who want to get their wishes heard. Politics should keep in tune with the human needs of the people.

These clues suggest a political orientation, a history of and antici- pation of immersion in conflict and compromise. However, we can see more directly how this propensity works in practice by turning to the chairman's pattern of actual behavior.

STYLE OF ACTION

Beyond their different rates of verbal communication, how do the active and passive chairmen differ in their styles of leadership? In Table V.3, the two categories are compared in terms of the four main types of interaction: positive and negative social-emotional comments, and questions and answers. The scores for the two categories of

TABLE V.3

Types of Communications Initiated by Active and
Passive Chairmen, in Relation to Their Group Averages

Type of Communication	Mean for Active Chairmen	Mean for Passive Chairmen	Difference	Number of Comparisons which Differ as the Means Do
Positive	2.0	1.2	.8	31 of 36
Answers	2.0	1.3	.7	36 of 36
Questions	2.9	1.5	1.4	33 of 36
Negative	1.8	1.0	.8	28 of 36

chairmen are the means of the ratios of the individual chairmen's scores to the average scores for their boards. In other words, the table shows how far, on the average, the active and passive chairmen deviate from the norms of their respective boards.

In all but the Questions category the active chairmen exceed the passive ones by about the same margin. The active chairman asks nearly three times as many questions as the average member of his group, while the passive chairman poses only one-and-a-half times as many questions as his group's average. Obviously the active chairmen are doing far more in the way of setting problems for their boards to discuss, polling members for their opinions, drawing out information, and so on.

Furthermore, the active chairmen address more of their comments to the group as a whole (rather than individual members) than do the passive. On the average they speak 36.5 per cent of their total comments to the whole group, as compared with 27.2 per cent for the passive chairmen, a relationship which holds for 27 out of 36 possible comparisons. In general, then, the active chairmen are presiding in a more definite way than the passive, and maintaining a focus on the group as a unit.

The apparent similarity between active and passive chairmen in Negative comments obscures a difference which emerges when the elements of this category are examined in detail. Negative social-emotional comments include expressions of disagreement (10), tension (11), and antagonism (12). In Table V.4, active and passive chairmen are compared in terms of the percentage of their total comments represented by each of these elements. The contrasts are small but fairly consistent: active chairmen disagree more and are more likely to express at least some antagonism. But the proportion of their com-

TABLE V.4

**Percentage of Total Comments in Three Negative
Social-Emotional Categories for Active and Passive Chairmen**

Type of Negative Comment	Mean for Active Chairmen	Mean for Passive Chairmen	Number of Comparisons which Differ as the Means Do
Disagreement	4.3%	3.1%	30 of 36
Tension	3.3	6.3	28 of 36
Antagonism	.5	.1	26 of 36

ments which express tension is only about half as large as it is for passive chairmen. Active chairmen appear, then, to enter into the group discussion somewhat more freely, while the passive are more restrained and tense.[3]

Another piece of evidence supports this interpretation: the active chairmen are more self-assertive in the discussions. Their average ratio of self-references (I, me, my, mine) to group-references (we, us, our, the board, etc.) is .64, compared to .47 for the passive chairmen, a relationship confirmed in 19 of 30 cases.[4]

[3]For related findings—e.g., that there is less tension in groups led by active, popular "great men"—see Edgar F. Borgatta, Arthur S. Couch, and Robert F. Bales, "Some Findings Relevant to the Great Man Theory of Leadership," in A. Paul Hare, Edgar F. Borgatta, and Robert F. Bales, eds., *Small Groups* (New York: Knopf, 1955), pp. 568-74.

[4]Individuals could not be identified in the typed transcript of one board.

A special problem for the chairman is handling his relationships with rivals. The group member who participates most can be either a challenger who competes with the chairman for attention and consent or an ally who supports him. Active and passive chairmen differ in the relationships they develop with the most active other participant. The active chairman is engaged in much more communication with his rival than is the passive chairman with his. On the average, in the active-chairman groups there is about 4.8 times as much communication between this pair as in the average pair for that group; the average between the passive chairman and the most active other is only 2.5 times as great as their group average; and the relationship holds for 30 of the 36 comparisons. Obviously the link between the active chairman and his most talkative colleague is much stronger than the link between the passive chairman and his rival.

A closer look at the content of the communication between chairman and most active member suggests a more interesting difference. Noting the direction of communication, we see that the active chairman speaks, on the average, 39.0 fewer comments to the highest other than the other speaks to him. Passive chairmen average 10.0 fewer comments, and this contrast between the chairmen in the two categories holds for 26 of the 36 comparisons. It appears, then, that the active chairman is less likely to respond directly to the challenger; rather he receives his remarks and then turns attention to other group members or to the group as a whole. The passive chairman tends to enter into a more evenly balanced exchange with the most vocal other member, and is drawn into direct colloquy with his rival.[5]

The chairman's authority may also be challenged by outsiders. During the last phase of the laboratory sessions which were devoted to an evaluation of the group's decision-making process, I participated in the discussion as an outside critic. My role was not very clearly defined, and it was not made clear whether I was taking over or leaving the chairman in charge. In this situation active and passive chairmen showed two interesting differences. First, the active chairmen attended to me about as much as they did to other members of their boards, while the passive chairmen went out of their way to address comments to me. This becomes evident when we compare the chairman's proportion of all remarks to me with his proportion of total group interaction for the day. The mean ratio of these two quantities is 1.05

[5]Cf. Barry E. Collins and Harold Guetzkow, *A Social Psychology of Group Processes for Decision-Making* (New York: Wiley, 1964), p. 96: "A group is most productive when it has a member who is uncontested in supervisory ability and/or decision-making approach."

for the active and 1.64 for the passive chairmen, and the individual comparisons are in this direction 32 out of 36 times. Clearly the passive chairmen were making a special effort to attend to the outsider, while the active chairmen treated me more casually, continuing to operate much in their usual style.

But the clearest difference emerged when I expressed direct criticism of each board. Near the middle of each of the evaluation sessions, I challenged the group in the following fashion:

> Let me press you a little bit here and be a little obnoxious about it. It sounds too good, it sounds too perfect; everything is fine, there's nothing that can be improved. Now is there anything at all in which you are less than perfect in your operation as a board of finance?

To this challenge, addressed to the group as a whole, all but one of the active chairmen responded immediately as spokesmen for their groups, defending and justifying their boards' performances. All but one of the passive chairmen let this opportunity pass: someone else stepped in to speak up for the group, while the chairman sat quietly by.

These bits and pieces of evidence fall into perspective when we look at the narrative material, particularly the transcripts of the boards' discussions as they worked on their budgets. Active chairmen took charge of the deliberations from the first, defining the problem, setting guidelines, surveying the members for their initial positions. "The first job is to get our feet on the ground," one began. "Well, fellows, we have a problem here," said another, and he then went on to spell it out. Passive chairmen sometimes tried to exercise initial control, but their suggestions were usually ignored. Active chairmen were more likely to ask for clarification from the experimenter before diving into details. Then the problem was to invent some simplifying approach to the problem: given restricted time, some system was needed to get quickly to the budget items which could be cut without hampering essential services. The least rational solution, going through the budget from the first item to the last, was attempted by several of the passive-chairmen groups, with the result that there was little time for systematic arguments for or against any one item. By contrast the active chairmen tended to insist on discussing and completing consideration of each proposal before moving on to the next.

These tendencies are highlighted by the deliberations of two fairly typical boards, one with an active and the other with a passive chairman. The passive chairman begins the problem by suggesting that the board follow its usual method of operation, going through the budget item by item. Note the fate of his proposals in the first stages of the budget-cutting exercise:

CHAIRMAN: We'll take the same procedure that we worked out when we worked in our own office.

M3: I'd like to ask one more question. This budget in total has been reduced already, and you want us to reduce it one more time?

BARBER: That's right.

CHAIRMAN: I have the original figures, and what we did reduce it. Start off with the selectman's budget — you have that?

M3: You want us to act just the same way as we do at home? Let's take $1000 off the selectmen's salaries.
(Laughter)

M2: [Speaking as First Selectman] I'll tell you gentlemen, if I'd taken the job for the salary, I would never have taken it!
(Laughter)

CHAIRMAN: We'll start off with the same procedure as we did when we did this originally. I'll read the items and if anybody has a question —

M6: Question, Mr. Chairman. What are you going to read there?

CHAIRMAN: Starting with the selectmen's budget.

M6: I think it would be rather important to know just why it is necessary to cut this $1000.

M3: Actually in this budget this year, we have one new item that actually we didn't use before: the capital expenditure of $10,000 for road equipment. . . .

At this point, the chairman has lost control of the procedure. Henceforward individual members chime in as the spirit moves them, skipping from item to item without completing the discussion of any of them. Eventually the deliberative process degenerates to a confused and unreasoning melee:

M8: I'll go along with Joe on that — I'm against that.

M3: I think we're kind of confusing —

CHAIRMAN: We should take the items as they appear —

M5: You're not using the same sheet that we are — we're using this sheet.

M2: We agree that temporarily drayage and livery is out. Secretary of the board of selectmen?
(Chorus of "out")

M2: Building inspector, car expense?
(Chorus of "out")

M2: Election expense is an unknown item — if no primary is called we might not necessarily need that amount; we could reduce it with the hope that —

M3: We're not talking monies — we've got to have election expenses.

M2: We don't necessarily have to have that much —

M6: Eliminate items —

M2: Clerk of the board of finance.
(Someone says "out")

M5: We gotta have a clerk
M6: For many years —
M1: I disagree with you. I think a clerk of some type has to be in there — part time.
M2: Then you're not eliminating it, but reducing it. We've eliminated drayage and livery so far. . . .

And so on. The chairman takes little part in the discussion and the group develops no satisfactory substitute for his control in directing the group's attention to one another and to specific tasks. No one clearly has the floor; no problem is posed for completion. Other members try from time to time to draw together a coherent group position, but, lacking the chairman's authority, these suggestions tend to get lost in scattered commentary.

By contrast, an active chairman begins the discussion of the "drastic" budget cut in this fashion:

CHAIRMAN: That's the problem: what is the bare minimum, what are the absolutely essential services that we've got to provide in order to keep the town in business?
M5: Well, it's pretty difficult without detailed —
CHAIRMAN: We've got the detail here. I would interpret this, just as a means of establishing our own ground rules, I would say that if you've got to be really drastic — this is not a suggestion, this is an *example* of something we might do. Take Rutledge Hall. Just for the sake of discussion you could close the hall and save all the expenses of operating that, janitor expenses and everything else, because you've got the schools where you can have town meetings and things like that.
M7: We can eliminate the parks, Memorial Day, cemeteries — none of those things are essential.
CHAIRMAN: Is it agreeable that we go on that basis?
M5: Well, that's the idea I had: absolutely essential, that would be the basis, eliminate the things that are not absolutely necessary for running the town.
CHAIRMAN: I just thought that we should have an agreement as to how we're going to approach this before we decide what [to cut].
M6: I'm not sure I understand, and I'm not sure I agree on it. I could sit here and say we don't need a fire department, and no one could argue with me because we don't need a fire department to run the town. There's no function of town government —
M5: I think that's stretching it a little.
M6: Who is to draw the line, who says —
CHAIRMAN: Common sense. We are by agreement, that's what we're about to tackle here.

From this point the board moves to consideration of various individual items thought to be less than absolutely essential. The chairman maintains his control over the proceedings, without, however, insisting that his substantive suggestions be adopted. He keeps the discussion focused on one problem at a time, finishing each before going on to the next. For example, to the suggestion that the board of finance could cut some of its own expenses, he responds:

CHAIRMAN: But remember that most of the board of finance expenditures are in here because under state law they've got to be done. The auditing in here has to be done by law. I don't know if we have to print the report up.
M5: Absolutely.
CHAIRMAN: That it has to be printed? All right, there's 575 and 600 – there's $1175 of that which by law we have to have in there.
M7: Then of course there's a certain amount of required advertising and so forth.
M3: So we could possibly save $175 there.
M1: No – If we had to we could cut out public health nursing –
CHAIRMAN: Board of Finance – you could probably take out $100 and get away with it. Is that agreeable – take away $100?
(General consent)

Here Member 1's attempt to move on to another topic (public health nursing) before finishing the one at hand (board of finance) meets the chairman's insistence on first getting group agreement on the board of finance item. The chairman is clearly on top of the procedure. Later in this discussion a member tries to raise again the question of the general approach to be taken; but the board had already decided that, and the chairman refuses to allow further consideration of the matter. And at the end he is the one who draws together a common position for the group.

To summarize the different styles of action displayed by active and passive chairmen, the data suggest that the active chairman works as follows:

1. He provides more directive procedural guidance for his group. He poses many questions, speaks more to the group as a whole, works to define issues, posits methods of attacking problems, maintains attention on each problem until it is resolved, and draws together a composite group decision.

2. He enters more freely into the give-and-take of group discussion of issues. The active chairman disagrees more and expresses more antagonism, but shows less tension. In the content of his remarks he is more likely to refer to himself than to the board as a whole.

3. He is less affected by rivals. He is less likely to be drawn into direct exchanges with the most active other member or to change his style in the presence of an outsider. But he does defend his board against direct challenges by an outside critic.

GROUP RESPONSE TO THE CHAIRMAN'S STYLE

What difference does it make how the chairman acts? Analysis of the data shows at least three areas in which the chairman has effects: (*a*) on communication to the chairman, (*b*) on evaluations of the chairman by other board members, and (*c*) on the integration and satisfaction of the group as a whole. Especially on the last point, the findings are not obvious.[6]

Table V.5 summarizes comparisons between active and passive chairmen in terms of communications received. As would be expected, the active chairmen stand out much more clearly in their groups as the recipients of many comments, collecting on the average nearly three times as many as the average member of their respective groups. The active chairman is clearly at the center of group interaction. Members other than the chairman address a smaller proportion of their remarks directly to the group as a whole in active-chairman boards (12.9 per cent) than in passive-chairman boards (15.6 per cent), a relationship holding for 26 of the 36 comparisons.[7] In other words, the active chairman is less likely to be bypassed.

Table V.5 also shows that in positive comments, answers, and questions received, the active chairmen exceed the passive by margins

[6]On reactions to leadership in small groups, see Sidney Verba, *Small Groups and Political Behavior* (Princeton, N. J.: Princeton University Press, 1961), chs. VI-VIII; Leonard Berkowitz, "Sharing Leadership in Small Decision-Making Groups," *Journal of Abnormal and Social Psychology,* XLVIII (1953), 231-38; D. G. Marquis, Harold Guetzkow, and R. W. Heyns, "A Social Psychological Study of the Decision-Making Conference," in Harold Guetzkow, ed., *Groups, Leadership and Men* (New York: Russell & Russell, 1963), pp. 61-62; Harold Guetzkow and John Gyr, "An Analysis of Conflict in Decision-Making Groups," *Human Relations,* VII (1954), 367-82; H. A. Landsberger, "Interaction Process Analysis of Professional Behavior: A Study of Labor Mediations in Twelve Labor-Management Disputes," *American Sociological Review,* XX (1955), 566-75; and Lawrence Schesinger, Jay M. Jackson, and Jean Butman, "Leader-Member Interaction in Management Committees," *Journal of Abnormal and Social Psychology,* LXI (1960), 360-64. Much empirical work on leadership has been done at Ohio State University: see, for example, Ralph M. Stogdill and Alvin E. Coons, eds., *Leader Behavior: Its Description and Measurement* (Columbus: Ohio State University, Bureau of Business Research, 1957).

[7]For related evidence that in business and government conferences, "the more the participants tended to talk to each other rather than the leader (and thus the less the behavioral leadership of the chairman), the higher the conflict," see Collins and Guetzkow, pp. 202-3.

of about the same magnitude (.9 to 1.2). But this is not the case for negative comments. The passive chairmen receive about as many negative reactions as we would expect on the basis of their over-all reception rates, but the active chairmen fall far below their expected level of negative reactions received. In response to many more initia-

TABLE V.5

Types of Communications Received by Active and Passive Chairmen, in Relation to Their Group Averages

Type of Communication	Mean for Active Chairmen	Mean for Passive Chairmen	Difference	Number of Comparisons which Differ as the Means Do
Positive	2.1	1.1	1.0	32 of 36
Answers	3.1	1.9	1.2	34 of 36
Questions	2.6	1.7	.9	30 of 36
Negative	1.4	1.5	−.1	19 of 36
Total receptions	2.8	1.7	1.1	33 of 36
Positive minus negative	.7	−.4	1.1	32 of 36

tives, the active chairman meets about the same amount of resistance, relatively, as does the passive chairman. This leaves him with a more comfortable margin of agreement received over disagreement received — one indicator of his influence over the other members. And while three of the active chairmen succeeded in getting one or more of their proposed solutions to the budgeting and board of education problems adopted formally by their groups, none of the passive chairmen's suggestions were adopted. In general, then, the active chairmen gain not only more attention and commentary from the other members, but also more assent and support.

Another aspect of support for the active chairman is revealed by close analysis of the group's behavior in his absence. As will be remembered, each chairman was called out of the laboratory after exactly fifteen minutes of the board of education discussion and returned exactly five minutes later. One effect of this procedure is remarkably consistent: when comparing interaction during the time the chairman was out and in the preceding five-minute period, in every one of the active-chairman groups the percentage of *negative* acts increases (by an average of 8.3 percentage points), and in all but one of the passive-chairman groups the percentage of negative acts decreases (by an average of 5.8 percentage points). In other words, when the active chairman is taken out the level of conflict in his group goes up; removing the passive chairman reduces conflict in his group. The picture is less clear for the five-minute segment following the chairman's return, but in four of the six active-chairmen groups negative comments decline (an average of 3.7 percentage points), and in four of the six passive-chairman groups negative comments rise (an average of 4.3 percentage points), indicating some tendency for the chairman's reentry to reestablish the climate which prevailed when he left.

How can we explain this apparent lapse into controversy when the active chairman leaves? And why does the passive chairman's absence reduce conflict? The data suggest two complementary explanations. Examination of the narrative content of the discussions suggests that when the active chairman goes out, other members of the group step in to check the chairman's main antagonist. Typically the chairman has been advancing or defending a position with considerable support from the group, but at least one member has been advocating an alternative proposal. When the active chairman leaves, his position is suddenly weakened — its organizing center is withdrawn — and the alternative position suddenly acquires advantage. At this point several of the chairman's allies move to his defense, making it clear that they oppose any retreat while he is away. The higher rates of disagreement result because the chairman's antagonist is attacked from several directions at once, as the members express their disagreement with his alternative.

In the passive-chairman groups a different picture emerges. Typically in the period before the chairman is called out, the discussion is rambling and confused. The group seems to be waiting for leadership, but the man who occupies the only formal leadership post, the chairman, fails to act. Other members hesitate to take over as long as he is physically present, but when he leaves the way is open for the emergence of informal leadership. Definite proposals, drawing together the strands of argument already developed, are advanced and gain agreement. In three of the passive-chairman groups (but in none of the active-chairman groups), the board actually reached a decision on the problem while the chairman was absent, and when he returned he was greeted with half-humorous, slightly denigrating remarks: "You're going to be outvoted — we've got a solution to this"; "While you were out that was our decision"; "We decided this — no, we didn't decide, we discussed."

Thus the decline in negative comments during the time the chairman was out appears to indicate the development of group consensus on substantive issues. Previously voiced objections are disposed of once the quiet chairman is no longer there to inhibit positive action by the group's informal leaders.[8]

---

[8]In this case the passive chairman, by occupying the position without performing the role, is a "task obstacle." See Collins and Guetzkow, ch. 3.

More direct evidence is available on the attitudes of members toward active and passive chairmen from questionnaires administered following the board of education discussion. A series of sociometric questions (Q21) asked members to vote for their first and second choices on six criteria:
Who contributes the best ideas for solving problems?
Who does the most to guide the discussion and keep it moving effectively?
Who helps the group to keep a friendly, pleasant atmosphere?
Who has the most influence with the other board members?
Who is liked best personally by you?
Who has the most personal initiative and ability?
Individuals are given two points for every first choice received and one point for every second choice received. Votes for oneself are excluded, and a score is computed as a ratio to an expected value, taking into account varying group size, votes for absent members, and abstentions.[9] Table V.6 compares the resulting scores for active and passive chairmen.

TABLE V.6
Scores on Six Sociometric Criteria for Active and Passive Chairmen

Criterion	Mean for Active Chairmen	Mean for Passive Chairmen	Difference	Number of Comparisons which Differ as the Means Do
Ideas	4.7	1.5	3.2	35 of 36
Guidance	6.5	3.9	2.6	28 of 36
Friendliness	3.6	2.5	1.1	22 of 36
Influence	5.4	2.7	2.7	34 of 36
Being liked	4.3	1.3	3.0	34 of 36
Initiative	3.4	1.4	2.0	23 of 36
Average Score	4.6	2.2	2.4	32 of 36

First it is clear that the active chairmen tend to achieve higher scores than the passive chairmen. The average score for active chairmen is 4.6 times that expected by chance, more than twice that of the

[9]Members could vote for others present or absent, for self, or abstain. The model assumes equal probabilities of voting and receiving votes; first choice counts 2, second choice 1. Expected value:

$$2 \times \frac{V_1}{N} \times \frac{1}{NG\text{-}1} \times (N\text{-}1) + \frac{V_2}{N} \times \frac{1}{NG\text{-}2} \times (N\text{-}VR_1\text{-}SV_1\text{-}1)$$

where N = number present; V_1, V_2 = votes cast on first and second choices; SV_1 and SV_2 = votes for self; NG = number of members, present or absent; VR_1 = votes received from others on first choice. For a review of findings on sociometric choices, see A. Paul Hare, *Handbook of Small Group Research* (New York: Free Press of Glencoe, 1962), ch. 5.

passive chairmen, and the active chairmen surpass the passive on each of the six criteria. As the right-hand column shows, these relationships are quite consistent in comparisons of individual chairmen, except perhaps on the Friendliness and Initiative items. Insofar as these six questions are tapping a generalized popularity among the members, the active chairmen appear to be much more highly valued leaders of their groups than the passive ones are.

The average scores for both categories of chairmen are highest on Guidance—"Who does the most to guide the discussion and keep it moving effectively?" Obviously this is the criterion most clearly associated with the chairman's role. But the active chairmen surpass the passive ones by a wide margin on this score, and by even wider margins on such task-facilitative qualities as contributing the best ideas and exercising influence. The active chairman receives more respect from his colleagues for these substantive contributions; he is also much more likely to be personally popular with the other members, as shown by the gap between active and passive chairmen on the Being liked scores. If his active leadership arouses any antagonism in the group, this is not reflected in the group's direct rejection of him as a person. Or perhaps the passive chairman, who receives his lowest score on the Being liked item, is even more likely to be rejected personally because he fails to perform the leadership functions expected of him.

However, on one criterion—"Who helps the group to keep a friendly, pleasant atmosphere?"—the difference between scores for active and passive chairmen is surprisingly small (1.1) and relatively inconsistent (it holds for 22 of 36 cases). The passive chairmen do slightly better than their average on the Friendliness item; the actives do considerably worse than their average. This is the first of several indications that the active chairman, despite generally superior performance as task leader and despite the direct respect and loyalty which his performance engenders in the members' minds, is rather less successful than might be expected in meeting the needs of the group for harmony and pleasantness. Four additional comparisons between active and passive chairmen support this interpretation.

1. There is a larger proportion of negative acts in the total communication of active-chairmen groups (where the average is 7.1 per cent) than in the passive-chairman groups (where it is 4.8 per cent), and this relationship holds for 27 of the 36 comparisons. The proportions of positive acts are about the same for the active- and passive-chairman categories, 13.5 per cent and 14.5 per cent respectively. Consequently, in terms of net agreement—one indicator of harmonious intragroup relations—the passive chairmen do better than the active ones.

2. Individual members of active-chairman groups are more likely

to see their goals as conflicting with those of their fellow board members. The questionnaires included four paragraphs (Q29a) describing sets of "goals of town government." Members were asked to pick the one "you would tend to stress most as an important set of town goals" and the one "most members of the board stress most." In the active-chairman groups, an average of 33 per cent of the members chose different goal descriptions on these two criteria. Only an average of 18 per cent of the members of passive-chairman groups saw their goals as differing from those of their boards. A relationship in this direction holds for 25 of the 36 comparisons.

3. Members of active-chairman groups appear to be somewhat less committed to continued service on their boards than are members of passive-chairman groups. Answers to the question, "How likely is it that you would be willing to serve for two or more future terms on the board of finance?" (Q12), were scored as follows: Definitely would, + 2; Probably would, +1; Probably would not, −1; Definitely would not, −2. Averaging these scores for each board gave a group score. Groups with active chairmen average .63 on this willingness-to-return item, while passive-chairmen groups average 1.11, a relationship which holds for 26 of 36 cases.

4. Members of active-chairman groups tend to rate their own performance on the laboratory tasks lower than do members of passive-chairman groups. The questionnaire asked for ratings of (*a*) the conclusions and (*b*) the methods of the group on each of the two main laboratory tasks, "reducing the budget" and "relations with the board of education" (Q1,2). Answers were scored as follows: Perfect, +3; Excellent, +2; Satisfactory, +1; Not-so-good, −1; Poor, −2; Very poor, −3. Group-average scores on these four questions range from 1.06 to 1.69. The active-chairman groups average 1.21, compared with 1.43 for the passive-chairman groups, and this relationship holds for 30 of the 36 comparisons.

These indications of interpersonal conflict, disagreement on goals, low satisfaction with group performance, and lack of commitment to continued membership in active-chairman groups as compared with passive-chairmen groups acquire significance when viewed against the background of the previously described findings. In absolute terms the passive-chairman groups are only somewhat happier and more harmonious than those with active chairmen. But given the active chairman's generally more effective performance and the more favorable evaluation of him by his colleagues, we might expect a finding strongly in the opposite direction. How is this apparent contradiction to be explained?

Two possibilities suggest themselves. First, the active chairman is making demands on his group that probably arouse a certain amount of negative feeling.[10] He makes proposals of his own and seeks consent for them; in this he may seem to take advantage of his position as chairman to advance his own personal viewpoint. He imposes restraints, insisting that the discussion be kept relevant and orderly. He presses for a decision as the group's time runs out. The members recognize the need for this leadership and grant the chairman credit for exercising it. But it is not unreasonable to assume that a certain amount of frustration builds up in reaction to these demands, and that it finds a way out in interpersonal conflict and dissatisfaction. The passive chairman engenders other kinds of frustration (particularly by holding leadership without exercising it), but at least he leaves the members alone.

A second explanation, equally plausible, reverses the hypothesized direction of causality: perhaps some chairmen are more active than others *because* their groups are less unified and satisfied. The chairman may well be responding to the atmosphere of the group as much as he is creating it. At the extremes, the chairman of a group in which the members are continually at one anothers' throats is under considerable pressure to intervene, while the chairman of a completely harmonious group may feel no particular need to do anything.

The present data offer no direct way to determine the relative influence of these two tendencies. Undoubtedly both contribute something to the response the active chairman elicits: an amalgam of attention, agreement, respect, and loyalty with a substratum of controversy and discontent. On balance, the data point strongly toward the active chairman as a major contributor to effective task performance, in contrast to the passive chairman, who occupies a leadership position without performing a leadership role. But the last set of findings — that groups in which the chairman leads are likely to be marked by more conflict and dissatisfaction — demands that we look more closely at the meaning and import of "integration" as a characteristic of these committees. If a group's power is to some degree a function of its unity, in what does its unity consist?

[10]Cf. Robert F. Bales, "The Equilibrium Problem in Small Groups," in Talcott Parsons, Robert F. Bales, and Edward A. Shils, eds., *Working Papers in the Theory of Action* (Glencoe, Ill.: Free Press, 1953).

CHAPTER VI

Integration and Interaction: The Power of Unity

A RECURRING THEME in the vast small groups literature is that a group which has the purpose of producing something encounters two fundamental problems: the efficient accomplishment of its work and its own maintenance as an integrated unit. These problems are usually seen as interrelated aspects of the same set of phenomena. That is, we observe the members of the group communicating with one another—the primary data—and then analyze this communication from a dual standpoint: how well does it function (*a*) to produce substantive results and (*b*) to hold the group together? Generally we think of success in solving either of these problems as contributing to success in solving the other. A well-integrated group produces better; productiveness encourages integration. However, as we saw in the last chapter, and as other researchers have noted, this simple paradigm does not always match reality. In fact, there are tendencies for the drive and discipline necessary for production to create frictions within the group, frictions which can, in turn, hamper and disrupt future performance.

What is rarely clear in studies of group decision-making is the appropriate meaning to be attached to "integration" in various contexts. Does it mean, for example, that the members of the group

    like one another?
    are similar to one another?
    hold common values?
    find membership rewarding?
    interact a good deal?

cooperate effectively on the task?
perform complementary roles?
expect and/or desire to continue as a group?
think highly of the group?
interact in "we" rather than "I" terms?
defend the group against external challenges?
have a stable and legitimate structure of relationships?
are willing to make sacrifices for the group?
express agreement with one another?
are happy?

Or are some of these elements appropriate for integration in some contexts and others in other contexts?

The problem of definition is extremely complicated, since, in social science, the term "integration" has been used to refer to several overlapping concepts; and research findings based on one may or may not hold for the others.[1] Yet it is undoubtedly true that integration is, in some sense, an important facet of group decision-making. This chapter does not solve the definitional problems but it will suggest, at least, what type of definition is likely to be most fruitful for research on the kinds of government committees represented by our boards of finance.

PARTICIPATION AND INTEGRATION

A remarkable experiment with amusing and significant results was conducted by Andie L. Knutson of the University of California.[2] Knutson wanted to find out (among other things) the effect on "membership satisfaction, group identification, and performance" produced by composing work groups of members with similar rates of participation. Graduate students in two laboratory courses in the School of Public Health at the University of California were first observed in their regular class sessions to determine which ones talked a lot and which ones said little. Subsequently four new groups were formed to bring together individuals who had participated with like frequencies: a "very vocal group," "vocal group," "quiet group," and "very quiet

[1]For a good introduction to the problem of defining and measuring integration or cohesion, see Dorwin Cartwright and Alvin Zander, eds., *Group Dynamics: Research in Theory* (Evanston, Ill.: Row, Peterson, 1953), ch. 7. Two political science studies which make extensive use of integration concepts are Richard F. Fenno, Jr., "The House Appropriations Committee as a Political System: The Problem of Integration," *American Political Science Review*, LVI (1962), 310-24; and Harold P. Green and Alan Rosenthal, *Government of the Atom: The Integration of Powers* (Englewood Cliffs, N.J.: Prentice-Hall, 1963), pp. 44-65. See also Ezra Stotland, "Determinants of Attraction to Groups," *Journal of Social Psychology*, XLIX (1959), 71-80.
[2]"Quiet and Vocal Groups," *Sociometry*, XXIII (1960), 36-49.

group." An effort was made to match the members of the groups on intellectual ability and other characteristics. Each group was required to draft a report on pretesting a pamphlet for public distribution by the California state health department. After three weeks of work, the students filled out questionnaires on the experience, and their reports were submitted, without any explanation of the nature of the groups or the experiment, to two top officials of the state health department for evaluation.

At the beginning of the initial meeting of the "very quiet group," no one spoke for fifteen minutes and "the first member of the group to raise a question concerning the task was looked to as leader." The "very vocal group" jumped into action immediately, the members offering a wide variety of suggestions. The other two groups—the "vocal" and "quiet" ones—were intermediate in their rates of participation.

After the experimental sessions were completed, Knutson's subjects were asked a series of questions designed to get at their reactions to their group assignments and their satisfaction with the whole experience. The results, arranged in frequency distributions for all four groups, show strong positive relationships between the vocality of the group and their happiness and satisfaction. Statistically significant at the .01 level were distributions on positive response to items dealing with one's own group membership, satisfaction with the group assignment, preference for one's own group, evaluation of the production of the group, and satisfaction with one's own participation. In other words, the more vocal the group, the more enthusiastic the members were about the process and results of their work. Narrative quotations from the questionnaires buttressed this finding.

Subsequently the four reports produced by the groups were put in similar wrappers and sent to the two judges in the state health department, who were asked to "rank the group reports in terms of the quality and usefulness of the product." The judges did not consult with one another, but their conclusions were quite similar. They are summarized in Table VI.1 which shows that, with one minor departure, the reports were ranked in reverse order to the groups' vocality. That is, the more talkative the group, the worse their product. The best reports were produced by the quiet groups—by those hesitant, unhappy, dissatisfied students who began haltingly and ended with the feeling that they had done poorly.

Knutson's experiment illustrates the complexity of relationships among participation, group integration, and effectiveness. Had the research concluded without the evaluation phase, the interpretation might have been quite misleading: it would have appeared that the vocal groups were "best" in some general sense, rather than simply more self-satisfied. Clearly, considerable caution is necessary in moving from observations on the general level of morale in a group to judgments about group effectiveness.

TABLE VI.1
**Knutson's Experiment: Judges' Rankings of Groups
in Terms of Quality and Usefulness of Product***

	Very Vocal Group	Vocal Group	Quiet Group	Very Quiet Group
Judge A	1	2	3	4
Judge B	1	2	4	3

*Highest ranking (4) indicates best quality and usefulness. Reprinted with the kind permission of Professor Knutson.

However, Knutson's research leaves intact a finding supported by much other research with a variety of small groups: the strong positive relationship between participation and member satisfaction. In the boards of finance research, we have no objective measures of group effectiveness, but we are prepared to test the hypothesis that the more one participates the more satisfied, integrated, and attracted to the group he will be. As a measure of participation, we have the ratio of each member's total number of acts initiated to the average for his group. And from the questionnaires and content analysis we can provide a number of indicators of satisfaction by transforming the answers to questions into scores for each individual. Table VI.2 gives the simple correlations between participation and ten different measures of satisfaction. The implication of these figures is evident: *there is apparently no relationship whatsoever between participation and satisfaction in the government committees observed for this study.* Members who say little in the discussions are just as likely to express satisfaction with the board as members who say much. No matter which of the ten measures of satisfaction or integration we look at, the correlations with participation are close to zero. For these groups, there is no evidence that being one of the more active members of the group makes one feel particularly happy as a member.

Perhaps, however, the talkative members *contribute* more to the integration of the group, even though they themselves are not especially pleased. We might expect that the talkers in a group would be

TABLE VI.2
Simple Correlations between Participation and Satisfaction Measures

Satisfaction Measures	Correlation with Group-Related Participation Rate
Rated importance of membership to self (Q23)	.05
Rated importance of board activity to self (Q18)	−.03
Willingness to continue as member (Q12)	.17
Rating of board's performance (Q17)	−.02
Rating of board's reputation among citizens (Q34)	−.09
Rating of board's reputation among officials (Q35)	.07
Reported proportion of friends in town government (Q40)	.03
Reported social interaction with other members (Q19)	.09
Conflict between one's own and group goals (Q29a)	.10
Ratio of self-references to group-references	−.02

perceived by their fellow members as the ones who hold the group together, as central members in comparison with the peripheral non-talkers. A look at relationships between participation rates (again considered as ratios of individual interaction to group averages) and sociometric ratings is revealing on this point.

As Table VI.3 shows, there is a general tendency for the active members to get more votes on sociometric criteria than the quiet members do, much as active chairmen exceed passive chairmen on this measure (see Chapter V). But it is also of interest that the lowest correlations are those between participation and the items measuring Friendliness (Who helps the group to keep a friendly, pleasant atmosphere?) and Being liked (Who is liked best personally by you?). Our interpretation of this finding will depend on the degree of association

TABLE VI.3
Correlations between Sociometric Ratings Received and Participation

Sociometric Ratings	Correlation with Group-Related Participation Rate
Ideas	.44
Guidance	.53
Friendliness	.31
Influence	.54
Being liked	.32
Initiative	.46
Average score	.53

we expect to find among these variables; but it is clear that keeping the group friendly and being likable are not the outstanding qualities related to participation.[3]

Another indicator of integrative or satisfaction-producing behavior might be the degree to which a member stresses positive thinking — agreeing, supporting others, and so forth — as a part of his total initiatives in the group, and, conversely, the degree to which he holds back expressions of disagreement. But on neither count do the high participants excel. In fact, the simple correlation between the participation rate and the percentage of total initiations which were coded as positive (agreement) is negative: —.24. Participation and the percentage of negative initiations (disagreement) are correlated —.12, that is, in the expected direction, but hardly significantly so.

The thrust of this evidence returns us to the initial set of findings: unlike the close linkage between participation and satisfaction or integration which Knutson found in his groups, the links between these variables in the boards of finance appear to be weak. How is this to be explained? I suspect that the problem lies, first, in the operational definition of participation which is used here, based as it is on a simple frequency count of communicative acts, and also in differences in the history and purposes of these government committees in contrast to those of the usual experimental group. Probably more important than the quantity of participation is the meaning members attach to it. The boards of finance are established groups, with the kind of slowly-developed, stable internal structure which the Knutson groups might eventually have developed. Over time the members come to expect and to accept marked differences among themselves in rates of participation. As they learn about one another, and their differences of ability and special knowledge become evident, they no longer rate themselves on how much they talk but on what they contribute, in the context of what is expected of them. Furthermore, the boards of finance have serious work to do; others outside the groups themselves are depending on them for careful, responsible action — they are not, in short, simply participating in an experiment. For both these reasons, it is the quality of his performance, considered in the light of his abilities, not how often he performs, upon which the member rates himself.

[3]On differentiation between task and social-emotional leadership, see Barry E. Collins and Harold Guetzkow, *A Social Psychology of Group Processes for Decision-Making* (New York: Wiley, 1964), pp. 196-200; on tendencies against such differentiation in permanent groups and those with unambiguous leadership, see A. Paul Hare, *Handbook of Small Group Research* (New York: Free Press of Glencoe, 1962), pp. 111-16. On relationships among participation, integration and effectiveness, see Sidney Verba, *Small Groups and Political Behavior* (Princeton, N.J.: Princeton University Press, 1961), chs. IX, X, especially pp. 232-43.

Thus there are members who say practically nothing in the discussions and yet feel just as integrated in the group as do the more active members. In one board of finance, two members remained silent throughout all the laboratory deliberations. At the end of the day, as the final evaluation session was drawing to a close, I asked each of them for a comment, to which they replied as follows:

M1: Well, I think the way they've been going along, they've been trying to do their best. I guess if they can get the selectmen to give them a clearer picture, they'll go further. Of course, I'm new on the board, only my second year.

BARBER: Any different problems that you see, other than the ones that have been mentioned?

M1: No, I'll go along with that.

BARBER: Mr. Doe?

M2: Well, I think the thing that you've done is really you've gained the confidence [of the townspeople]. They're old swamp Yankees, and I mean, you can't change them — but you have changed them that much. In any field, I think, our county is a world of their own, I don't care how you look at it. They're all independent. And [an official] is one of the old school. Once you've won him over, which I think you have — I know you have — this thing will straighten itself out as far as these books and figures. And actually today there is no real big problem outside of getting this figure out of them. Once that's straightened out, which I think it will be, I don't think there's any problem.

These two full-fledged members speak of the board of finance in the second or third person — as "they" and "you" rather than "we." They comment as if they were spectators casually observing someone else make decisions. And yet they are not alienated from or critical of the board. Both give a strong positive evaluation of the board's work in the above quotations. Both report on their questionnaires that the board does "very well" in living up to its purposes and that being members of the board is "very important" to them. One notes that he "probably would" be willing to continue on as a member, while the other says he "definitely would." In short there is no indication that these silent members, who have passively observed their colleagues talking all day, are in any way less attracted to their group than the others are.[4]

Considering these particular indicators of "integration" as dependent variables and frequency of participation as the independent varia-

---

[4]On acceptance of differentiation of roles, see Theodore M. Newcomb, "An Approach to the Study of Communicative Acts," in A. Paul Hare, Edgar F. Borgatta, and Robert F. Bales, eds., *Small Groups* (New York: Knopf, 1955), pp. 158-60.

ble, we find no clear relationship between them. Apparently the hypothesis that participation leads to satisfaction and/or attraction to the group needs to be modified for the particular kinds of groups studied here by inquiring into the meanings of both participation and integration in a different way.

REWARD AND INTEGRATION

Perhaps we have been looking at the matter backwards. Instead of expecting a sense of satisfaction and feelings of attraction to the group to be related to something the member gives — participation — we might reasonably view it as a result of what the member *gets* from the group. Stated generally, the hypothesis would be: the more rewarding the experience in the group is for the individual, the more integrated he will feel. At least four kinds of reward are pertinent.

1. Receiving Agreement. The member will feel rewarded if the other members of the group express agreement to him. He should come away from a meeting in which he has received a good deal of agreement more satisfied than if he has received little agreement. As a measure of this variable we can use the percentage of all comments a member receives in the agreement category (Bales categories 1, 2, and 3).

2. Avoiding Disagreement. The member will feel rewarded if the other members of the group do not express disagreement to him. He would prefer to be agreed with, but if his moves receive neutral responses, that is better than if they receive negative responses. As a measure we can use the percentage of all comments received in the disagreement category (Bales categories 10, 11, and 12).

3. Receiving Attention. The sheer amount of communication directed to a member may be defined as a kind of reward. The other members direct their comments to him; he is not ignored. If the attention of the group is a scarce commodity which cannot be equally distributed, the member who gets much of it may feel rewarded. As a measure, we can use the total number of comments a member receives, as a ratio to the average for his group.

4. Receiving Respect. Perhaps the interaction measures above are too crude to catch the types of reward most meaningful to a member. Another dimension is added when we consider the reputation he attains in the eyes of other members. To what degree do they give him their respect? As a less-than-perfect measure, we can use the average sociometric score a member receives, lumping together the ratings he gets for ideas, guidance, friendliness, influence, likeability, and personal initiative (Q21).

As indicators of integration, we can select those from the list above (Table VI.2) which seem to aim most directly at the member's satisfaction with and attraction to the group, namely, the importance he attaches to his membership, his probable intention of continuing as a group member, his rating of the board's performance, and his tendency to refer, in his remarks, to the group rather than to himself. Table VI.4 shows the correlations between these two sets of variables, reward and integration.

A look at Table VI.4 shows that all but a few of the correlation coefficients are near zero—and that the few which may be statistically significant point in the wrong direction! That is, for example, the larger the proportion of agreement a member receives, the *less* importance he attaches to his membership, the *less* willing he is to return, and the *less* he tends to refer to the group rather than himself. Possibly the more

TABLE VI.4
Correlations between Reward Measures and Integration Measures

| Reward Measures | Integration Measures | | | |
	Importance of Membership	Willingness to Continue	Rating of Board's Performance	Self-References/ Group References
Percentage of agreement received	−.27	−.25	−.02	.24
Percentage of disagreement received	.18	.11	.00	−.02
Interaction received/group average	.07	.11	.04	−.13
Average sociometric score received	−.07	.09	−.05	−.12

disagreement a member receives the more important he feels being a member is—a strange and inexplicable clue. Much as in the case of the non-relationship between participation and integration, we find here that *there is apparently no relationship between rewarding experiences and integration in the government committees observed for this study.* Members who are left out in sociometric ratings, disagreed with, and ignored in the deliberations are just about as likely to be attracted to and satisfied with the group and their place in it as are the sociometric "stars" at the center of the conversation. In fact, in some cases the rewarded members may feel even less integrated than the other members do.

Here again, the reason for these unanticipated negative findings probably lies in the lack of fit between our measures of reward and the ways the members interpret the comments they receive. On the one hand, over time groups may develop structured expectations about the distribution of rewards, so that individual members vary considerably in their anticipations of receiving various kinds of rewarding messages. In a newly-formed group of people who do not expect to continue to interact far into the future and who are not confronted with important work to do, frequencies of approval, attention, and respect may be taken as indicators of reward. But to understand the meanings of reward in a group with long experience, anticipations of extended future interaction, and significant tasks — in other words, with a developed internal culture — we need to take a closer look at the ways members perceive their relationships with one another.

INTERNAL GROUP CULTURE

"We had a good discussion, but we all arrived at the same thing." This remark by the chairman of one board of finance as his group reached the end of the board of education problem summarizes the central feature of the internal culture of these committees. In all but one of the twelve groups, members reached a unanimous decision on this "hot" topic. The analyst attempting to explore intragroup alliances and conflicts through voting records would have no material to work with. In the course of discussion there is often considerable controversy.[5] But by the time the group gets down to making a final decision, the conclusion is almost always in this form:

CHAIRMAN: All right, all in favor of the proposal?
ALL: Aye.
CHAIRMAN: Opposed?
(Silence)
CHAIRMAN: Carried.

The kind of group integration represented in this conclusion is developed through discussion. In no case do we find unanimity from the first; every group displays at least some differences of opinion when the problem is presented. The internal integrative process, like the process of developing relationships with other groups, is governed throughout by a set of norms, a culture composed of certain values defining the proper tone and character of the deliberations. As revealed in the evaluation sessions, these values are usually negative: they state what the group does not and should not do as it goes about reaching a unanimous decision. Examination of these norms helps to show why

[5]Cf. the exchange above, pp. 54-55.

integration in these groups is more than a matter of participating and being agreed with.

1. Controversy does not reflect political partisanship. This theme could probably be broadened: controversy does not reflect any loyalties to specific external groups other than the whole community. But it is most clear that the members continually downgrade the importance of partisanship—the differences among them which might disrupt their unity most severely, since they owe their membership on the board to nomination by political parties and might be expected to feel some sense of responsibility toward these organizations. The following comments are typical:

> M4: Well, I'd say, as I said before, I defy anybody to sit down at any of our meetings and determine, without knowing beforehand, who's a Republican and who's a Democrat. I think it would be impossible.
> M2: Politics is never brought into it.
> M4: I think we're all interested in the town and that's what we're viewing.
> M2: Unless it was a wisecrack or something like that.
> M7: As far as any politics goes, it's absolutely without any party.

Or as another board put it:

> M6: We don't consider the political aspects of it, either.
> M3: No, this is definitely a non-political board in spite of the fact that we're selected—
> M6: It's the most non-partisan board I have ever sat with.
> M3: No voting along political lines; as a matter of fact, if we didn't wear badges you couldn't tell one from the other (laughs).

This theme is repeated in almost every one of the board of finance discussions. "Even though we are split politically, that's beside the point." "We started off on the board being non-political and we've tried to keep it that way." "We don't feel that we're members of the party when we sit in there."

In terms of group integration, this non-partisan stance means that controversy does not engage feelings of responsibility and commitment beyond that to the community as a whole—at best a rather amorphous and inarticulate group. One need not feel that he is on the board to represent particular interests, with all that that would imply. The member is free to change his mind without feeling that he has let his party down. Partisan politics is dangerous to the unity of the group. By continually denying its significance, the boards of finance foster the kind of flexibility of opinion which makes final unanimity possible.

2. Controversy does not involve personal animosity. A search through the transcripts of the problem-solving sessions reveals very few occasions in which members express anger at one another in a clearly personal way. They do not hesitate to disagree with one another, but they very rarely lose their tempers. As one member says of controversies on his board:

I don't think they are unhealthy, or serious. I mean, in other words I think — let's put it this way: by the time the evening is over, I think the controversy is forgotten. I think that each of us respects the other person's view and his right to express it as vehemently and as strongly as he wants to, and I don't think we consider personalities a problem.

Or as a member of another board says:

Let's put it this way: we never get vicious. I don't think we've ever hurt anybody on the board, but we do get, sometimes, very wrapped up in it.

This norm of impersonality in debate is probably one of the most widespread common values among legislators generally. It means that disagreement is not perceived as threatening to the respect and affection members have for one another. Controversy can be heated, but the heat is directed toward the substance of the argument, not toward the person who advances it. The fact that substantive issues are resolved — decided and then left behind — both results from and contributes to the maintenance of affectional ties among members. Fights — never "taken personally" in the first place — end, leaving intact the integrated group.

3. Unanimity does not indicate passivity. Controversy is impersonal, but its subject matter is not unimportant. Individuals are expected to express their opinions frankly and openly rather than simply falling into line with the first suggestion advanced. The "ideal member" of a board of finance is nobody's pawn, but a person with his own ideas and a determination to get them heard. As one chairman says:

My response to your comment and suggestion that we might not be critical enough is that I would accept that, except that from experience I know that the several members of the board of finance are such a hardheaded, independent, individual crop of people. They are completely individual and independent personalities. And fortunately they're all very articulate indeed. I think that we're critical enough.

A member of another board says, "Everybody speaks his own mind, what he thinks should be, and he isn't afraid to do so and is expected to do so by everyone else." And a voice from another group adds, with a laugh, "There are no bashful members on this board."

The important feature of participation as a factor in group integration is thus not that everyone talks a lot, but that everyone feels free to express his opinion. Members are not expected to participate at the same rate, but to participate without restraint when they have something to say. The final outcome of the deliberative process is thus neither abject surrender by the defeated contenders nor passive acquiescence due to timidity.

The important point behind these norms is that controversy and integration are not opposites in the deliberative process, but rather factors which complement and support one another. Controversy is possible because the group has defined it in a particular way, channeled it into productive courses. Integration thus includes agreement on the norms by which this defining and channeling is accomplished. Conversely, integration in the sense of unanimous agreement on practical solutions in which the members have confidence is made possible by controversy, by the working through of many objections to the proposal the group finally adopts.

Two statements from members of different boards summarize these themes. The first illustrates best an emotional attachment to the group and its process; the second presents a rather sophisticated elaboration of approximately the same ideas:

I don't know—Maybe I'm patting this board of finance on the back, but in the years I've been on this board, it's been a pretty close working board, in that each member seems to come there with—he's already found out some of the problems he's going to have with whatever issues are coming up, or he's gone to search out public attitude. We sit down at the meetings and the chairman has always called on anyone that is the head of the department which is involved, or any appropriate—in other words, we seem to function pretty well. I don't know, I think we are an ideal board. I know I'm speaking very freely but, we have our arguments, we have our discussions, and there are times when I know I myself take a different attitude than the other members. But then again, you wouldn't need a board of finance if you didn't have different attitudes. And we still come out—we're walking out, we all feel that we've done a job. You've got your disagreements, you've got your opinions, yet there is a conclusion, and to the best of my knowledge I've never seen the taxpayer hurt on any of the conclusions.

Don't you feel, Bill, that the unanimity comes more from the exhaustive analysis of the problem and the resolution of our conflicts? Really, I think that we tend to turn things down where, perhaps, if they weren't given this criticism they would be accepted. But we've had complete turnabouts in the same evening. We don't reach this unanimity because any of us are too bashful to get up and state our views. What went on here today is nothing compared to what goes on in some of our regular executive sessions when we have real hot problems. But I think we do make a conscientious effort to resolve these questions and we do come up with reasonable solutions. The essential part of democracy is of course this give and take that occurs trying to reach a reasonable solution. It doesn't mean a compromise of principle; we've never compromised principle. We've presented alternative plans to be used, and I think out of these alternative plans we've usually come up with a favorable decision for the town. So the difference is between not being critical enough and resolving the problems because you *have* been critical, and that's where I think our board gets its greatest strength.

For the boards of finance, then, integration depends less either on expressive opportunities as such or on receiving many positive responses than it depends on a particular kind of interchange among persons as they perform their tasks. The emphasis is on the job to be done.

TASK INTEGRATION AND PATTERNS OF INTERACTION

This emphasis on the *work* of the board, as opposed to frequencies of participation and reward, is reflected to some extent in correlations between two indicators of task performance and the four indicators of integration used above. In the questionnaires, members were asked, "How would you rate your own performance so far on the board of finance?" (Q13), and "Compared with most other board members, how much influence do you feel you have on board decisions?" (Q23). The answers were scored and correlated with the four integration indicators to produce Table VI.5. The relationships are uneven — with 85 respondents it takes a correlation coefficient of about .25 for statistical significance at the .01 level[6] — but there is clearly a connection, of an order of magnitude different from those encountered so far, between the feeling that one has influence over the substantive decisions the board makes and his integration and/or satisfaction in the group. And a high rating of one's own performance appears to be associated with a high rating of the board's performance and a sense that membership is important to one, although not with willingness to continue or a tendency to stress the group rather than the self.[7] These figures hint at relationships which might have been stronger if our measures were less crude. The variations we are dealing with in these responses are shadings of enthusiasm for the board and positive estimates of influ-

[6]Using the "Z" statistic. See Hubert Blalock, *Social Statistics* (New York: Mc-Graw-Hill, 1960), pp. 305-7, 456-57.
[7]For evidence that "success on the group task will produce satisfaction," see Collins and Guetzkow, pp. 196-200.

ence and performance. Negative responses are rare: distinctions between such favorable alternatives as "excellent" and "fair," "very well" and "fairly well," "slightly more influence" and "somewhat more influence," "probably would" and "definitely would," are difficult to evaluate. The truth is that the great majority of the members of these

TABLE VI.5
Correlations between Task-Performance Ratings and Integration Measures

Integration Measures	Task Performance Ratings	
	Rating of One's Own Performance	Rating of One's Own Influence on Decisions
Importance of membership	.38	.22
Willingness to continue	.10	.32
Rating of board's performance	.26	.22
Self-references/group references	−.03	−.21

boards report positive feelings about their work and the board itself. For this reason, it makes more sense to explore how the members go about their work in a descriptive way, than to try to explain the minor differences among them in a comparative way.

Here we will focus not on the individual member but on relationships among members. The problem is to see how the actual internal communication of the group is organized, in terms of patterns of interchange. The significance of this kind of data can be illustrated from the Knutson experiment with quiet and vocal groups.[8] The superiority of the quiet groups' products, despite the less than satisfying performances of individuals, was largely due to their success in relating to one another in a productive way. Their reports "reflected an organized and interrelated approach to the gathering of essential data and to the drawing up of pertinent conclusions." The very vocal group, in contrast, failed to develop any coordinated decision-making system: their report revealed "the degree to which competition for leadership and individual expression must have influenced its group process." No one in the very vocal group had even read the finished version of their report, which contained a page of personal observations by each member. In other words, the quiet-group members, while *less* effective as individuals, were *more* effective as a group than were the vocal-group members. The crucial difference was in the relationships members developed with one another.

The Bales Interaction Profile Analysis data for the boards of finance deliberations provide evidence for exploring two significant

[8]Knutson, p. 45. See above, pp. 102ff.

features of internal communication. The first of these we might call the *concentration* of interaction within the group. We already know that some members initiate a good deal more interaction than other members do, and that some receive more than others. But beyond this unevenness in individual participation rates, there is unevenness in rates of exchange between members. That is, a member does not distribute his remarks equally to each other member of the group: he addresses more of his remarks to some members than to others. Similarly, a member receives more comments from some sources than from other sources. What determines these special relationships within the group? Why do we find Members *X* and *Y* communicating frequently with one another, to the neglect of Members *A, B*, and *C*? Posed in another way, how can we explain the structure of communication flows within these groups?

Secondly, we can move beyond the analysis of gross interaction flows to focus on relationships among our four different kinds of communication: agreement, disagreement, answers, and questions. Are there observable tendencies for these elements of discourse to fit together in patterned ways, that is for *integration* of interaction. Do some members specialize in initiating and/or receiving one or more of these varieties of comment? What tendencies are there for certain kinds of initiatives to evoke certain kinds of responses?

Together these two lines of inquiry should produce a statistical profile of the ways members relate to one another as they go about making their joint decisions.

CONCENTRATION OF INTERACTION

As a first step in exploring concentrations of interaction, we need to sort out several distracting aspects of communication between individuals. Suppose, for example, that we find Member *X* initiating many comments to Member *Y,* in comparison with the interaction between other pairs of members. This does not necessarily indicate a special relationship between *X* and *Y*. *X* may simply be a talkative person who communicates often with every member of the group, including *Y*. On the other hand, *Y* may be a favorite target for remarks, one to whom every member of the group talks a lot. The high rate of communication between *X* and *Y* could thus represent nothing peculiar to their relationship, but simply their individual tendencies toward loquacity and receptiveness.

Furthermore, our groups are of different sizes. For comparability from group to group we need to allow for the differences this implies in the expected rate of communication between individuals. Thus if we were to find, say, 25 per cent of X's comments going to Y in a group of five, and 10 per cent of A's comments going to B in a group of nine, we would not be justified in attributing a closer relationship to the pair X-Y than to the pair A-B. The higher rate of interaction in the first pair may be due simply to the smaller number of sources and targets for communication rather than to any peculiarity of the interpersonal relationship.

To control for these extraneous factors, we can make use of a measure developed by Deutsch and Savage,[9] and Alker[10] for the analysis of international trade: the "Relative Acceptance" or RA. This RA expresses for any pair of members, i (initiator) and j (receiver), the degree to which the actual volume of communication from i to j exceeds or falls short of the volume expected on the basis of the size of the group, i's total initiation rate, and j's total reception rate. A positive RA thus indicates a surplus of communication from i to j over what we would predict, and a negative RA indicates a dearth of communication. In this sense the RA is a measure of concentration of interaction, isolating a clearly special feature of i's relationship to j, the extent to which i goes out of his way to talk to j.

As discussed so far, the RA is a one-way measure – that is, it describes communication from one member to another member. To characterize the *exchange* of comments in the pair, we can use the sum of the RA's, or $RA_{ij} + RA_{ji}$. This provides a characterization of the concentration of interaction in a given pair, disregarding the direction of the interaction. This will highlight the pairs in which one or both members are deviating from the amount of communication predicted for them.

Now we might hypothesize that an excess of interaction in a pair would be due to certain similarities between the two members. The more educated ones might prefer to talk to one another rather than to the less educated, for example. Or those of about the same age might interact more frequently, ignoring those who are younger or older. These tendencies would then reinforce the impact of particular variables on the decision-making process; for example, social class would be emphasized if members tend to communicate primarily with others at the same class level.

On the other hand, interaction might concentrate in pairs of

[9] I. Richard Savage and Karl W. Deutsch, "A Statistical Model of the Gross Analysis of Transaction Flows," *Econometrica*, XXVIII (1960), 551-72.
[10] Hayward R. Alker, Jr., "An IBM 709 Program for the Gross Analysis of Transaction Flows," *Behavioral Science*, VII (1962), 498-99.

members with different characteristics which complement one another and stimulate communication. For example, members of different political parties might engage in extra communication as they work out their policy differences, the old might instruct the young, and so on. These relationships of reciprocity or complementarity could supply the dynamic tendencies of interaction, imparting movement and development to the deliberations.[11]

In order to test these ideas, a series of social distance measures was derived for each of the 273 pairs of members in our twelve boards of finance. The absolute difference between each member and each other member of his group was calculated for the following variables:

(1) Age (Q53)
(2) Education (Q58)
(3) Income (Q60)
(4) Self-identified social class (Q59)
(5) Years of residence in the town (Q51)
(6) Seniority: years of membership on the board (Q6)
(7) Party identification, as measured on a scale of intensities ranging from "Very Strong Republican" to "Very Strong Democrat" (Q24,25)
(8) Party choice, a simple dichotomous variable indicating whether the two members belong to the same (0) or different (1) parties (Q24)
(9) Personalism, as measured on a scale of preferences for warm, close relationships with others versus cool, distant relationships (F1)
(10) Outside contact. This is the *sum* of scores by the two members of a pair on their reported frequency of seeing and talking with each other on occasions other than board meetings (note that this is an indicator of closeness, not distance) (Q19)
(11) Participation. The ratio of the member's total comments to the average for members of his group

In Table VI.6, the correlations between these eleven "distance" measures and the concentration measure (sum of RA's) are reported. The first thing to notice in this table is the general lack of correlation between concentration of interaction and those variables which we would have expected to determine it. Apparently communication between paired individual members is not affected in any regular way by their similarities or differences in age, education, income, class,

[11]Cf. John W. Thibaut and Harold H. Kelley, *The Social Psychology of Groups* (New York: Wiley, 1961), ch. 3.

years of residence in town, strength or direction of party loyalties, or social connections. The impact of these variables on the content of decision-making is not reinforced by the structure of specialized participation flows within the group. Put more simply, we do not find the oldsters or the rich, the Republicans or the well-educated, the friends or those who consider themselves upper class either favoring or avoiding one another in any consistent way. There is a slight tendency

TABLE VI.6
"Distance" Measures and Concentration of Interaction:
Correlations for 273 Pairs of Board of Finance Members

Distance Measures	*Correlation with Concentration of Interaction* $(RA_{ij} + RA_{ji})$
Age	−.05
Education	−.01
Income	.00
Self-identified social class	.01
Years of residence in town	.07
Seniority	−.11
Party identification	.04
Party choice	.00
Personalism	.21
Outside contact	.07
Participation	−.18

for differences in seniority to depress frequencies of interaction below that expected, but while this relationship (−.11) is undoubtedly statistically significant, given 273 cases, it is not particularly strong.

But the two largest correlations in Table VI.6 provide interesting hints regarding the structure of interaction in pairs. There is a significant negative relationship (−.18) between (*a*) differences in participation rates and (*b*) concentration of interaction. That is, there is some tendency for members whose over-all frequencies of interaction are similar to interact more with one another than would be expected. When a member selects (probably unconsciously) another member as the "target" for his remarks, he is likely to choose someone who participates about as much as he does, the quiet ones addressing remarks to other quiet ones and the more vocal ones sending a surplus of comments to those who also talk a lot. Since we know that the sociometric ratings are rather strongly related to participation rates, it is probably true that these groups tend to be stratified to some extent in terms of both participation and status *within the group*. The effect is perhaps to "layer" the discussion on the basis of criteria specific to the experience members have with one another in the course of working on their board of finance problems. Other status differences, based on characteristics achieved or ascribed outside the group, appear to have little bearing on the concentration of interaction.

The second interesting correlation is that between (*a*) differences in personalism scores and (*b*) concentration of interaction, the coefficient being .21. The farther apart two members are on this warm-cool dimension, the more likely they are to go out of their way to talk to one another. Thus while similarity in participation rates appears to engender concentration of interaction in a pair, *complementarity* in this personality dimension has this effect. This is not due to any general tendency for the more outgoing personalities to participate more. For individuals, the correlation between personalism and participation is an insignificant .06, and that between personalism and participation received is .03. For pairs of members, the correlation between personalism distance and participation distance is −.06. In other words, it is the *relationship* between individuals with complementary orientations toward social intercourse (personalism) that trips off a higher-than-expected rate of communication, and this effect is independent of that produced by similarity of participation rates.

The meaning of this complementarity is not hard to fathom. The member who is warm and outgoing, who "will go out of my way to make people like me," and for whom "sharing experiences and being partly responsible to others is very important," tends to interact with the cooler, more withdrawn and task-oriented member, who agrees that "in a group I don't get involved with personalities but prefer to stick to what we're supposed to be doing." The interplay of these characteristics stimulates interaction, keeps the discussion moving as the members react to one another.[12]

To explore this topic further it is necessary to move beyond the analysis of over-all interaction counts in order to consider relationships among different kinds of interaction.

INTEGRATION OF INTERACTION

Group integration can be considered as the patterned ways by which individual members fit their interactions together to produce decisions. This fitting together can be described in its general outlines

---

[12]On effects of personality homogeneity and heterogeneity, see Collins and Guetzkow, pp. 100-106. William G. Schutz has findings which do not support the complementarity hypothesis; see *FIRO: A Three Dimensional Theory of Interpersonal Behavior* (New York: Holt, Rinehart and Winston, 1960), pp. 128-35.

by analyzing correlations among subcategories of participation, although in so proceeding we sacrifice a great deal of detail. Working with frequencies of acts, we neglect intensities of meaning. And by moving back from the substantive issues the members are discussing, we see configurations which they might consider peripheral or irrelevant. The interpretation of this evidence is fraught with difficulty. Even the fundamental distinction between stimulus and response as elements of integration is never entirely clear: an expression of agreement, for example, may be taken as a response, but it is also in some sense a stimulus, an initiative, to which the person agreed with responds. What we can get from analysis of interaction counts is some indication of general tendencies, the drift of interaction, the flow of conversational particles which underlies the decision-making process.

The first and most basic proposition about integration is simply that initiatives tend to be reciprocated. Considering each individual's participation as a ratio to the average for members of his group, initiatives are correlated with receptions at .84. Obviously there is a strong tendency for members to direct their remarks to those others who initiate a lot—and/or for members who receive much interaction to respond at a like rate. Undoubtedly forces are at work in both these directions. The result is a pattern of interchange which is organized around a few central members of the group and characterized by mutuality rather than one-way communication. The leading members in terms of initiatives do not preach to a passive congregation; they communicate, primarily, with one another.

To move beyond this general characterization we can look first at relationships among types of initiations, then among types of receptions, and finally between types of initiations and types of receptions.

Table VI.7 shows correlations between initiation rates and the composition of initiations, in terms of the proportion of each of the four types of comments. It is evident that the more one participates the larger the proportion of Answers (suggestions, opinions, information) in his comments. The more active members tend to specialize in

TABLE VI.7
Initiation Rate and Four Types of Initiations

Types of Initiations	*Correlation with Group-Related Initiation Rate*
Percentage of agreement	−.24
Percentage of answers	.31
Percentage of questions	−.23
Percentage of disagreement	−.12

121

conveying task-oriented, problem-solving attempts, while the less active put more emphasis on agreeing and asking questions, on what might be called facilitative contributions. Disagreement, on the other hand, has the weakest relationship to participation rates.

This pattern is further clarified when we look at intercorrelations among individuals' proportions of the four kinds of comments, as displayed in Table VI.8. Here the large negative correlations between the proportion of Answers in a member's initiations and the other types show a tendency toward considerable specialization in that one category. That is, the person who concentrates his comments in the

TABLE VI.8
Correlations among Four Types of Initiations

	Percentage of Agreement	Percentage of Answers	Percentage of Questions	Percentage of Disagreement
Percentage of agreement	——	−.78	.22	.01
Percentage of answers	−.78	——	−.64	−.39
Percentage of questions	.22	−.64	——	−.02
Percentage of disagreement	.01	−.39	−.02	——

Answer category tends to do so at the expense of all other categories, particularly Agreement and Questions, while those who initiate heavily in the other categories tend to send out lower proportions of Answers.

The other correlations in Table VI.8 show again a positive relationship between the percentage of Agreement and the percentage of Questions. In other words, the same individuals are likely to initiate a high proportion of Agreement and of Questions, at the expense of Answers, while the person who initiates few Questions also initiates few acts of Agreement. The relationship of these categories with Disagreement is random—there is no clear tendency for the Agreement specialist to avoid disagreeing with others, or for the questioner to take a critical (disagreeing) role.

The pattern of initiation roles emerging from these correlations can be summarized as follows:

1. Problem-Solving Role. The individual specializes in giving suggestions, opinions, and information for the solution of the group's substantive problems.

2. Facilitative Role. The individual specializes in agreeing and in eliciting suggestions, opinions, and information by asking questions.

3. Critical Role. This is less clearly defined than the other two. The individual who specializes in disagreement does so at the expense of positive problem-solving attempts, but he does not show any regular tendency to express a lower proportion of Agreement than other members do, and he is no more prone to ask questions. The meaning of this finding remains obscure at this point.

Turning to patterns of reception, Table VI.9 shows relationships between individual reception rates and the composition of receptions,

TABLE VI.9
Reception Rate and Four Types of Receptions

Types of Receptions	Correlation with Group-Related Reception Rate
Percentage of agreement	−.30
Percentage of answers	.44
Percentage of questions	−.25
Percentage of disagreement	−.19

again in terms of the proportion of each of the four types of comments. Here the correlations among categories follow closely those we have already seen for initiations. The more one receives, the larger the proportion of Answers in his total receptions. The person who receives few comments (relative to the average for members of his group) gets a higher proportion of Agreement and Questions, and, perhaps, Disagreement.

Intercorrelations among the four kinds of receptions are shown in Table VI.10. The first thing to notice in this table is the general lack of large positive or negative numbers. That is, relationships among proportions of comments received are less definitely structured than are those among comments initiated. The only relationships which appear strong are those with the percentage of Answers received. The person who gathers in a large proportion of Answers does so pri-

TABLE VI.10
Correlations among Four Types of Receptions

	Percentage of Agreement	Percentage of Answers	Percentage of Questions	Percentage of Disagreement
Percentage of agreement	——	−.11	.01	−.07
Percentage of answers	−.11	——	−.41	−.33
Percentage of questions	.01	−.41	——	−.10
Percentage of disagreement	−.07	−.33	−.10	——

marily at the expense of Questions and Disagreement received. Put another way, he is just about as likely as anybody else to receive a high or low proportion of Agreement, but less likely to receive high proportions of Questions or Disagreement.

Beyond this there is no indication that roles as receivers are well-defined in these particular groups. For example, if we know the proportion of Agreement a member receives this does not help us much in estimating the proportion of Answers, Questions, or Disagreement he gets. In order to understand the dynamics of interchange we must move to relationships between patterns of initiation and patterns of reception.

Table VI.11 shows more clearly how proportions of initiations and receptions are linked. The following hypotheses are supported:

1. The larger the proportion of Agreement one initiates, the larger the proportion of Questions he receives.
2. The larger the proportion of Answers one initiates, the larger the proportion of Agreement he receives.
3. The larger the proportion of Questions one initiates, the larger the proportion of Answers he receives.
4. The larger the proportion of Disagreement one initiates, the larger the proportion of Disagreement he receives.

TABLE VI.11

Correlations between Four Types of Initiations and Four Types of Receptions

| | Receptions | | | |
| | Percentage of Agreement | Percentage of Answers | Percentage of Questions | Percentage of Disagreement |
Initiations				
Percentage of agreement	−.21	.16	.24	−.19
Percentage of answers	.35	−.23	−.10	−.06
Percentage of questions	−.36	.41	−.09	−.16
Percentage of disagreement	−.06	−.23	−.03	.67

THE CHARACTER OF INTEGRATION

What clues do these findings give us about the nature of integration in the boards of finance? They can be interpreted as indicating norms or patterns of expectations about the responses appropriate for various kinds of initiatives. And they lead into speculations about the consequences for integration of violating such norms. In the long run, members of these groups probably acquire habits of interaction, learning what to expect when they proceed in a certain fashion and how they in turn are expected to deal with certain kinds of comments which come their way.

Thus the person who sends out a high proportion of Agreement in his initiations can expect to receive a high proportion of Questions. He is not relegated to a passive, responsive role: his suggestions, opinions, and information are requested. In this way, the particularly agreeable character is brought into the substantive discussion. His reticence (see negative correlation with initiation rate) is in part overcome as the other members draw him out, perhaps because they anticipate his general agreement with their ideas. Working groups in which the more agreeable members receive other types of response might well leave these participants in the role of yes-men, simply acquiescing in whatever is suggested to them.

The person who specializes in giving Answers can expect to receive a high proportion of Agreement. This of course has the effect of encouraging the flow of ideas, feelings and facts, increasing the available alternatives from which the group can finally select its answer. A poorly integrated group in this sense would be one in which the proliferation of proposals is blocked by excessive rates of disagreement, or in which the proposals advanced are very often poor ones which call for rejection. In general, the norm of the boards of finance appears to be that one offers ideas which are good enough to elicit agreement.

The questioner gets Answers. The complementarity or reciprocity involved here is evident: the group tends toward integration when questions are raised which can be, and are, answered. Members are motivated to seek help in moving toward a mutually satisfactory solution of their problems when and if help is available. The group which lacks the resources needed to answer its questions is poorly prepared to get its work done.

Finally, the member who gives out a high proportion of Disagreement is very likely to receive the same in return. The contribution this relationship makes to group integration is somewhat obscure, but it is at least evident that the challenger is challenged, that the group's eventual unanimity is not based on acceptance of any objection which happens to be raised. Controversy is not lost in a fog of neglect or surrender — there is confrontation and argument on the way to resolution.[13]

[13]Cf. Robert A. Dentler and Kai T. Erikson, "The Functions of Deviance in Groups," *Social Problems*, VII (1959), 98-107; Robert C. North, Howard E. Koch, Jr., and Dina A. Zinnes, "The Integrative Functions of Conflict," *Journal of Conflict Resolution*, IV (1960), 256-74; and George A. Theodorson, "The Function of Hostility in Small Groups," *Journal of Social Psychology*, XLIX (1959), 71-80.

What these findings suggest is that the analysis of "integration" in these government committees (and probably in similar part-time, on-going work groups) is unlikely to be fruitful if it is focused primarily on measures of *general* satisfaction or personal reward. Participation in these committees — both in terms of membership and of speaking out in meetings — is voluntary; morale is generally high. Perhaps satisfaction and reward variables would be more useful for the study of groups in which the members are either less fully committed to the group (so that interpersonal feelings have a more determinative effect on relatively casual interaction) or much more fully committed to the group (so that interaction is more significant for individual happiness).

But at least for the part-time boards of finance, the central focus of integration is on task interaction, on the ways members relate to one another as they work toward a decision. Particularly by mapping out relationships in the exchanges of questions and answers, of suggestions and consent, and the inquiring and critical modes of discourse, the outlines of a dynamic system of integration are clarified.[14]

Within this system, individuals influence one another — but that is a matter for another chapter.

[14]Cf. George C. Homans, "Social Behavior as Exchange," *American Journal of Sociology,* LXII (1958), 597-606. For a finding, based on observations of 72 conferences in business and government, that "more adequate communication," "more orderly . . . treatment of topics," and "a more penetrating attack on the problem," contributed significantly to group productivity, while "cohesiveness," as measured primarily in affective terms, did not, see D. G. Marquis, Harold Guetzkow, and R. W. Heyns, "A Social-Psychological Study of the Decision-Making Conference," in Harold Guetzkow, ed., *Groups, Leadership and Men* (New York: Russell & Russell, 1963), pp. 62-64.

CHAPTER VII

Dimensions of Interpersonal Power

OBVIOUSLY SOME MEMBERS of a committee are more powerful than other members. Obviously, that is, until we try to specify in some precise way what it means to say that Member A is more powerful than Member B. The word "power" has a ring of intuitive plausibility about it; without much hesitation, we sense the gist of such phrases as "the power of the purse," "presidential power," "power play," "balance of power," "separation of powers," and so forth. Folk wisdom warns that "power corrupts," that there is danger in "the power behind the throne," and somehow we know what "you can't beat City Hall" means.

Yet almost as soon as one attempts to put these intuitive meanings into words, a host of complexities arise, as if one had uttered an incantation and summoned forth a thousand devils.[1] For example, suppose power is taken to mean the ability to bring about change in the activity of another person. Suppose further that we adopt the following operational definition: If A acts and then B changes, A has power over B. Immediately the following—and many, many more—questions can be raised:

---

[1]For some examples of theoretical formulations of influence, see especially Robert A. Dahl, "The Concept of Power," *Behavioral Science,* II (1957), 201-18; James G. March, "An Introduction to the Theory and Measurement of Influence," *American Political Science Review,* XLIX (1955), 431-51; James G. March, "Measurement Concepts in the Theory of Influence," *Journal of Politics,* XIX (1957), 202-26; and William H. Riker, "Some Ambiguities in the Notion of Power," *American Political Science Review,* LVIII (1964), 341-49.

1. Did *A* want *B* to change in this way? If not, we might mistakenly attribute power to a blundering oaf whose efforts bring down disaster on his head.
2. Would *B* have changed even if *A* had not acted? If so, we might err in attributing power to a busy but irrelevant bystander.
3. Does *B* resist *A*'s attempt to change him? If not, we might be calling a man powerful who can make another do something about which the latter is fundamentally indifferent, as in the solicitation of votes for corresponding secretary of a lodge.
4. Does *A* obligate himself to *B* as the price of persuasion? If so, we might be according power to a man who has placed himself in bondage to an opponent.

The complexities are far too numerous to be taken account of in any single conceptual formulation. And once we move beyond theory to research design, the number of plausible and semi-plausible operational definitions is staggering, and their links with theory are inevitably tenuous. Those who restrict themselves to activities which can be directly observed and/or quantified may miss phenomena which the actors themselves see as crucial to the power situation, such as the beliefs and feelings and attitudes attached to particular actions. But the researcher who is willing to take his subjects' word for it – to ask the actors who has how much power in a given situation – may mistake opinion for reality.

What is the way out of this dilemma? One method is to give up: power is too nebulous and too difficult to measure to be useful in political analysis. Just as the psychologists do not waste their efforts trying to define and measure love, so political scientists should not spend themselves on elaborate attempts to capture the essential meaning of power. The trouble with this argument is that it is nearly impossible to discuss decision-making without, at some point, introducing some variant of the concept of power. As soon as the door is opened for the concept of effectiveness or influence or authority, all the ambiguities of power sneak back in. Political science without power would be something like physics without gravity – a somewhat barren body of data.

An alternative way out is to select arbitrarily that one definition of power (at either the conceptual or the operational level) which best fits the researcher's intuitive notion of the essential quality of power. Thus one analyst will focus on the ability to inflict deprivations, another on the possession of resources, another on gaining rewards, another on winning contests. Each goes his own way with his own definition, conducting his own type of research and defending his conceptualiza-tion against those who see the essence of power differently. The problem with this solution is, it seems to me, that a great deal of time and talent is wasted in an essentially sterile argument about what power *really* means or about the one way in which it is best measured. The fact that different methods elicit different findings is a matter of concern only so long as one insists that there is some single method which would produce the only true findings on power.

A different explanation is that the phenomenon itself is many-sided, that it has a multitude of aspects rather than a unitary essence. In that case the problem is to investigate those aspects considered signifi-cant, or possibly significant, in a particular research setting, and to see how they are related to one another and to other variables. With this approach the apparent contradictions among findings represent op-portunities for further exploration rather than occasions for surrender or trench warfare.

No single research project can span the entire range of possible power definitions. This chapter, drawing on the questionnaires, interac-tion counts, and transcripts of the board of finance deliberations, (*a*) describes 45 operational definitions of interpersonal power, (*b*) shows how they tend to be reduced empirically to a few basic dimensions when applied to these data, and (*c*) examines the effects of some independent variables (such as socioeconomic status) on the main power measures. These measures all refer—some directly, some indi-rectly—to the *exertion* of power, that is, to power manifested in activity rather than power held in reserve.[2] Thus I treat resources such as seniority and socioeconomic status not as measures of power but as possible determinants of power. I am aware, however, that many other indicators have been developed and that the ones used here may operate quite differently in different research contexts.

The analysis of these data is fairly complex; few of us can keep in mind as many as 45 new variables for long. For this reason, the reader may prefer to look first at the summary of findings beginning on page 146, and then refer back to the more detailed definitions which turn out to be significant. Those familiar with factor analysis may want to skip immediately to Table VII.2, on page 145, to get a statistical picture of

[2]See Barry C. Collins and Harold Guetzkow, *A Social Psychology of Group Processes for Decision-Making* (New York: Wiley, 1964), pp. 152-53, and Georg Karlsson, "Some Aspects of Power in Small Groups," in Joan Criswell, Herbert Solomon and Patrick Suppes, eds., *Mathematical Methods in Small Groups Processes* (Stanford, Calif.: Stanford University Press, 1962), p. 193.

the main dimensions. But for a more complete view of the findings, one needs to begin at the beginning and grasp the main idea behind each set of definitions.[3]

LEADERSHIP ROLE

The formal position of chairman is clearly marked off in these groups. The chairmanship is also a role, although, as we have seen, the expectations which other members and the chairman himself attach to this role may be ambiguously defined. On the one hand, the chairman lacks the clear authority of a "director" or "chief." On the other, the chairman is something more than a "moderator." At a minimum, however, the chairman is the one member who is in some sense responsible for the conduct of the group; he is, at the least, expected to entertain and act upon formal motions and to manage relations with outsiders. Unlike the other members, the chairman seems to have a right to take the floor at any time. Thus our first operational definition of interpersonal power is simply

Definition 1. Chairmanship.

The score on this variable is 1 for each chairman and 0 for each other member.

POWER RATINGS BY OTHER MEMBERS

Sociometric ratings of power may reflect at least two significant aspects of the situation in long-lived groups such as our boards of finance. First, answers to the question, "Who has the most influence with the other board members?" (Q21), can be taken as estimates by reporters (members) who have had an opportunity to observe relationships among members over a long period of time. Their experience surpasses ours; they have watched for years what we have seen for a few hours. Insofar as reactions to the laboratory environment distort normal group processes and individual performances, reports by the members themselves may be more accurate than those of strangers observing the group make only a few decisions.

---

[3]In addition, for purposes of interpersonal power analysis I have eliminated data for six subjects, attending with various boards, each of whose status was somewhat ambiguous. These were minor town officials such as treasurers and secretaries, who, while they generally participated freely in the deliberations (and were thus members in the concrete sense used here), might not be expected to influence others in quite the same way as the regular members do. This reduces the N for the various computations in this chapter from 85 to 79; on balance, I think that the clarity of power status which this assures is worth the loss.

Secondly, and here the problem becomes more complex, the members may respond to one another not on the basis of some *objective* power situation but rather on the basis of *subjective* perceptions of power. In other words, if *A* thinks or feels that *B* is powerful, then he is apt to act as if *B* were powerful, whatever the facts of the case. Or, viewed from the group perspective, if *B* has managed to acquire a reputation for power, this in itself may lead other members to conform to his wishes.

As will be recalled, the questionnaires included six sociometric questions (Q21), which were labelled Ideas, Guidance, Friendliness, Influence, Likeability, and Personal initiative. First and second choices were elicited on each criterion; the person chosen for first place was assigned two points, and for second place one point. Votes for oneself were excluded, and the score computed was a ratio to an expected value, taking into account varying group size, votes for absent members, and abstentions. Of these six questions, the Influence item is obviously the one most directly related to interpersonal power. But each of the other five can also be interpreted as tapping some aspect of the exercise of power, in that each reports on the achievement of some goal the member may value. Furthermore, a look at correlations between Attributed influence and other sociometric scores, displayed in Table VII.1, reveals a tendency for a person rated high on Influence also to receive high ratings on the other items and on an average score for all six items. Since the correlations between (*a*) Attributed influence and (*b*) Friendliness and Being liked are somewhat lower than might be expected, there is some possibility of differentiating between task leadership and social-emotional leadership—a finding in accord with many other small groups studies.[4] In order to check on relationships

TABLE VII.1
Correlations between Attributed Influence and Other Sociometric Items

Sociometric Items	Correlation with Attributed Influence
"Who contributes the best ideas for solving problems?"	.83
"Who does the most to guide the discussion and keep it moving effectively?"	.75
"Who helps the group to keep a friendly, pleasant atmosphere?"	.36
"Who is liked best personally by you?"	.58
"Who has the most personal initiative and ability?"	.70
Individual's average score	.87

[4]See Collins and Guetzkow, pp. 214ff., and A. Paul Hare, *Handbook of Small Group Research* (New York: Free Press of Glencoe, 1962), ch. 5.

between these ratings and other power indicators, we will include all of them, as follows:

Definition 2: Attributed influence
Definition 3: Attributed best ideas
Definition 4: Attributed guidance
Definition 5: Attributed friendliness
Definition 6: Attributed likeability
Definition 7: Attributed initiative and ability
Definition 8: Average attributed leadership

SELF-DESCRIPTIONS REGARDING POWER

It would be facetious to say that no one is closer to what a man does than that man himself. But it is probably true that most people, most of the time, attend to their own actions more than anyone else does. Self-perceptions are notoriously subject to bias — but so are the perceptions of others. By including self-ratings we will at least be able to explore relationships between them and other indicators of power. For example, the correlation between the first of the self-ratings (*Definition 9* below) and Attributed influence (*Definition 2* above) is a respectable .40, although this may represent nothing more than agreement in error. But clearly one aspect of power relationships is the perceptions the actors have of their own power, taken, like the socio-metric ratings, either as reports by experienced observers or as subjective orientations toward power.[5]

The first of these items results from the question, "Compared with most other board members, how much influence do you feel you have on board decisions?" (Q23). Answers were scored as follows: Much less (1), Somewhat less (2), Slightly less (3), Slightly more (4), Somewhat more (5), and Much more (6). This I call

Definition 9: Self-rating on influence.

The remaining self-ratings are responses to questionnaire items drawn from William G. Schutz's FIRO-2 ("Fundamental Interpersonal Relations Orientation"), a personality test which involves choosing among various self-descriptions. The complete versions of these questions are given in Appendix C. For

Definition 10: Desire to be leader,

members were asked to rank their desires to be "very well liked," "a

---

[5]For a study using 25 self-ratings on influence, see George Levinger, "The Development of Perceptions and Behavior in Newly Formed Social Power Relationships," in Dorwin Cartwright, ed., *Studies in Social Power* (Ann Arbor: University of Michigan Press, 1959), ch. 6.

leader," and "prominent in the activities," "when I am in a group" (F5D). The scores on the "leader" alternative were as follows: third rank (1), second (2), first (3).

The form of the questions on which the next four definitions are based was the same: two paragraphs were presented and the respondent was asked to choose "which one comes closer to describing your average behavior." While degrees of emphasis can be expressed—i.e., the answer categories are in the form Slightly, Somewhat, or Much more like A than B—the major fault line is obviously between the two main alternatives. The answers are simply dichotomized in the middle to produce a (0,1) score.

A pair of paragraphs (F2) posed the difference between (*a*) dominating others in a markedly directive fashion when in a leadership role, instructing them on their duties and seeing to it that "the task is carried out according to the rules laid down," and (*b*) a looser, more permissive leadership style, in which "the most important thing to me is to try to include those who are working with me in the decisions and the responsibility I have," through discussion, compromise and agreement. Scored in the same way, this produces

Definition 11: Dominance as leader.

Power can be exercised not only in dominating others but also in resisting domination. The man who habitually stands up to the pressures for compliance exerted upon him maintains a kind of defensive power even though he may be completely unable to persuade others. A pair of paragraphs (F3) bearing on this variety of power contrasted types of responses in the follower role: (*a*) an insistence on knowing why one is asked to do something, on presenting "my arguments to the organizer" in case one has objections, "even if it perhaps delays the task, because I feel no one has the right to ask people to do something without giving reasons for it," as against (*b*) a willingness to carry out "instructions," even if one has objections, because it is likely that the organizer "knows what he is doing or he wouldn't have been put in charge." I think the title,

Definition 12: Resistance as follower,

catches the main meaning of this distinction.

I have also included in this collection of self-descriptions the "personalism" item used previously (F1). This contrasts a relatively cold, impersonal, independent set of orientations toward other people with a warm, outgoing, other-directed orientation. The power aspect here is not entirely clear, but one suspects that the gregarious person who tries "to make friends as quickly as possible with virtually everyone I meet" would be more persuasible than the staid fellow who tries "to keep my relations with people on a fairly impersonal basis." Thus, *Definition 13: Independence in social relations.*

Participation rates are often used as indicators of power.[6] The person who talks a lot in the course of group decision-making both demands and obtains the attention of his fellow members. (In a group of five or ten where one person speaks at a time it is difficult to avoid attending to the speaker.) In this sense the active members of the group "dominate the discussion," "hold the floor," "make themselves heard." At a minimum, the active ones manage to get their ideas before the group in greater volume than the passive ones. Among our self-descriptions is one (F4) counterpoising (*a*) taking "a very prominent part" in group discussions, staying "in the limelight," being "almost always one of the highest participators in any group," and (*b*) not trying "to participate very much," preferring to "sit back and listen," perhaps not participating in groups "as much as I should." A simple dichotomization of answers to this item gives

Definition 14: Normal participation.

So far, then, we have formal position (i.e., the chairmanship), perceptions by others, and self-perceptions. All of these are indirect indicators of power, included because they suggest inferences about power behavior. The remaining definitions are derived much more directly from observations during the laboratory sessions. They refer not to feelings or second-hand reports but to the members' actions; in this sense the data are objective. But the reasons for selecting certain indicators require argument.

SUCCESS

To the tough-minded power analyst, the difference between winning and losing may be the key indicator of interpersonal power. "Don't bother me with how they feel," he may say, "tell me who got his way in the end." Implicit here is the assumption that power is essentially, or at least importantly, a matter of initiating proposals which are later adopted. Simple and commonsensical as this sounds, it involves, of course, all the ambiguities with which we began and more. Yet as one aspect of interpersonal power it obviously has a place.

Two of the problem-solving tasks, cutting the budget by $1000 and adopting a proposal for board of finance – board of education relations, lent themselves to this purpose. Unlike the broader budget-cutting

[6]For an example of interaction counts as indicators of influence in a natural setting, see Sidney Rosen, "Effects of Adjustment on the Perception and Exertion of Social Power," in Cartwright, ch. 5.

134

problem, both of these problems typically elicited from a particular member a fairly clear suggestion for a particular solution that was later adopted, almost always unanimously, by the whole group. Thus any member could propose none (0), one (1), or two (2) of the solutions eventually agreed to.[7] This scoring provides

Definition 15: Winning proposals.

From this point on the definitions are based on Interaction Process Analysis counts. This means that power scores are calculated by various combinations of *frequencies* of acts. A critical underlying problem in this sort of analysis is that it necessarily equates each act of a given kind with each other act of a given kind, disregarding entirely variations in emphasis, substantive importance to the discussion, deviation from group opinion, and so on. Thus, for example, the statement "I agree 100 per cent with absolutely everything you say," and the statement, "I'm inclined to think you might possibly be right on this particular point," are both scored as Agreement and enter into the calculations as if there were no difference between them. The *Winning proposals* definition catches the significance of suggestions—these were the ones the board adopted as major solutions for the problems. Frequency counts, however, offer a different kind of information. They delineate the general drift of power relationships within the group, the adding up of many microscopic observations (some 27,000 of them) to produce a picture of power from a variety of angles.[8]

OBSERVED PARTICIPATION RATES

We have already included, in *Definition 14,* a report by each member on his usual rate of participation in groups. IPA data enable us to add two objective interaction scores. First, we have the individual's total number of acts initiated, taken as a ratio to the average number of initiations per member for his group. This item has behind it some of the same uncertainties and justifications as does reported participation, except, of course, that the scores do not depend upon the member's perception of his own behavior. Taking account of the way this variable is calculated, it can be called

Definition 16: Group-related initiations.

Participation is not only a matter of initiating acts, however. In

---

[7] This resembles one of Dahl's operational definitions, except that vetoes are not scored here. See Robert A. Dahl, *Who Governs?* (New Haven, Conn.: Yale University Press, 1961), pp. 332-33.

[8] For an analysis of some of the shortcomings of frequency counts, see Robert Golembiewski, *The Small Group* (Chicago: University of Chicago Press, 1962), pp. 99ff.

some sense simply being in the group, listening to and thinking about what is being said, is a type of participation. But there is probably little variation among members in this regard – although some may pay closer attention than others – and in any case we have no data on it. We do know, however, to whom each remark was addressed. By dividing the total number of acts a member receives by the average receptions for members of his group, we get a standardized reception score for each individual. Why is this an indicator of power? Perhaps because it shows whom the others consider worth talking to, who has the ability to gain and hold the group's attention, who is the focal point for the discussion. The high receiver is at least not ignored. Other members may be addressing many remarks to him because they feel his approval is necessary or helpful for getting their ideas accepted. Or perhaps they perceive him as representing the entire group. Another way of looking at a high reception rate is to see it as an indicator that the member's questions and suggestions elicit much response; that his ideas receive consideration, stimulate thought and discussion. Thus we include

Definition 17: Group-related receptions.

IPA coding also produces counts of comments according to twelve categories. For the remaining scores, these twelve are first collapsed to the four more general categories we have been using: Agreement (categories 1, 2, and 3), Answers or Suggestions (4, 5, and 6), Questions (7, 8, and 9), and Disagreement (10, 11, and 12). The Questions category will be ignored, as its power meaning is at best quite uncertain. (A question may indicate dependency, as when I request something from you, or dominance, as when I demand that you give me something.) To facilitate description of the variables based on these breakdowns, the following notations will be used:

P = Participation, that is, total comments

A = Agreement

D = Disagreement

S = Suggestions

i = initiated

r = received

Fundamental to all the definitions which follow is the concept of power as *gaining consent*. We assume that the objective of each member is to get the other members to agree with him. The more agreement he receives, the more powerful he is in the board of finance. In these committees, where final decisions are almost always made by unanimous vote, acts of agreement can perhaps be considered as micro- or mini-votes, cast along the way to a final solution. The need for a variety of measures derived from this concept springs from the variety of ways in which it can be interpreted. As will soon be clear, at least five basic types of distinctions are necessary.

VOLUME OF AGREEMENT RECEIVED

The simplest measure is the total number of acts of agreement an individual receives in the course of the group discussions. Suppose we imagine a member reviewing his experience after a board of finance meeting. He might well carry away an impression of his power in terms of the tendency of other members to agree with him, as indicated roughly by the number of agreements he received, regardless of other aspects of the experience. Thus we can include the following definition (the relevance of the vocabulary will soon be evident):

Definition 18: Raw agreement received = A_r.

PROPORTION OF AGREEMENT RECEIVED

But of course a member receives comments other than agreement. His ploys may elicit opposition, questions, counter-proposals, and the like. Furthermore, he may receive relatively few remarks from other group members, but rate his power on the proportion of agreement in the mixture of remarks he *does* receive. For example: "Nearly every response I received was positive," or "They gave me nothing but trouble." To represent this type of power estimate we can use

Definition 19: Percentage of agreement received = A_r/P_r.

NET AGREEMENT RECEIVED

In the definition above the volume of agreement received is considered in relation to everything the member receives. Thus the person who receives many comments would discount the significance of the volume of agreement he gets, while the person receiving few comments would inflate that quantity. But another way of discounting or inflating is (*a*) to eliminate from consideration all neutral responses (Questions and Suggestions) and (*b*) to concentrate on the *margin* of positive over negative responses received. That is, the individual may say to himself such things as "They agreed with me a lot, but they also disagreed with me a lot" or "I did not get much agreement, but at least they didn't oppose me much." Power may be defined in this sense as the excess of agreement received which remains after the disagreement

137

received is subtracted. In effect the measure cancels out one act of agreement for every act of disagreement received. The definition is

Definition 20: Net raw agreement received $= A_r - D_r$.

Now, without introducing too much more complexity, both of the discounting/inflating operations described above can be brought to bear simultaneously in the same measure. The member may use as his basic power estimator the net raw agreement received, but interpret this in the light of the total comments he receives. Thus he could say, "Of the comments I got, more were positive than negative," or "I received more support than opposition, but most of what I got was neutral." This combination provides

Definition 21: Net percentage of agreement received

$$= (A_r - D_r)/P_r.$$

Notice that in the formula for this definition a high volume of interaction received tends to depress the value, so that the more neutral comments (Questions and Suggestions) a member receives the less power he has by this measure.

BATTING AVERAGE

So far our agreement-based definitions have focused strictly on what the member receives, on the rewarding types of interaction he gets as the group converses. Nothing has been said of what he attempts. Yet a member (or his colleagues, or a political scientist) might well rate his power as success in getting consent in the light of the number of suggestions he makes. In this sense if two members get the same amount of agreement but one makes few suggestions and the other makes many suggestions, the former is more powerful than the latter. Thus a member may give his wife a postmeeting report in the form, "Every idea I proposed got support," reserving to himself the fact that he proposed very little. Just as it might be considered reasonable to estimate a congressman's power by the proportion of bills he introduces that pass, so we might use a "batting average" of this sort to rate the board of finance members.[9] Using both gross and net terms for this concept, we get

Definition 22: Raw batting average $= A_r/S_i$

and

Definition 23: Net raw batting average $= (A_r - D_r)/S_i$.

[9]On batting-average measures, see Collins and Guetzkow, p. 171; Robert F. Bales, *Interaction Process Analysis* (Reading, Mass.: Addison-Wesley, 1950), pp. 167ff; T. M. Mills, "Power Relations in Three-Person Groups," *American Sociological Review*, XIX (1953), 351-57; and Herbert Goldhamer and Edward A. Shils, "Types of Power and Status," *American Journal of Sociology*, XLV (1939), 171-82.

SURPLUS POWER

It seems nearly impossible to analyze power without introducing analogies. One which has found some favor takes off from the idea of exchange in group interaction to explore the "power economy" within the group. For example, if we had some quantifiable data on the topic we might be able to see how members accumulate power "credit," how the "interest rate" on power changes, how values are attached to various power "currencies," and so forth. Our interaction counts can be used to explore one of the simpler aspects of the economic model, the cost of power. The question is, "How much does a member have to pay to get consent?"[10] Does he get more than he gives? Or, more precisely, how much more or less does he get than he gives? In a horse trade, we may congratulate both parties on their new mounts, but we accord extra kudos to the man who got the better of the bargain. Similarly (to a degree), a member who can gain a great deal of positive response from others without "paying" them much positive response is in this sense powerful. The man who receives little agreement, on the other hand, may nevertheless be considered to have *retained* power if he has agreed little with others. Again, the person who gains consent for a high proportion of his suggestions while offering consent to a low proportion of the suggestions he receives raises his power. These cost considerations point to a concept of surplus power, defined, in the light of our previous distinctions, in the following four ways:

Definition 24: Surplus raw agreement received $= A_r - A_i$

Definition 25: Surplus percentage of agreement received
$= A_r/P_r - A_i/P_i$

Definition 26: Surplus net raw agreement received
$= (A_r - D_r) - (A_i - D_i)$

Definition 27: Surplus net raw batting average
$= (A_r - D_r)/S_i - (A_i - D_i)/S_r$

GROUP-RELATED MEASURES

The perceptive and patient reader will have noticed that none of the agreement-receiving power definitions described so far takes into account variations from group to group.[11] Yet it is clear that in some

[10]On cost aspects of influence, see especially John Harsanyi, "Measurement of Social Power," in Martin Shubik, ed., *Game Theory and Related Approaches to Social Behavior* (New York: Wiley, 1964), pp. 183-206; and John W. Thibaut and Harold H. Kelley, *The Social Psychology of Groups* (New York: Wiley, 1961), ch. 7.

[11]See Collins and Guetzkow, p. 96; and Josephine Klein, *The Study of Groups* (London: Routledge & Kegan Paul, 1956), p. 119.

groups power in the defined senses may be easier to come by than in other groups. Group size may make a difference: *a priori* we would expect a member of a large group to receive fewer comments of any kind than a member of a smaller group. There may be cultural differences among our different boards of finance, so that in some of them almost every proposal elicits a positive response, while in others most ideas are challenged. In order to allow for these possibilities, "group-related" scores were computed for all but one (percentage of agreement received) of *Definitions 18* through *27*, by dividing the individual's score by the average score for members of his group. This process produces nine additional definitions, listed below for later reference. The formulas are simply those of the original variables divided by the appropriate group average score:

> *Definition 28: Group-related raw agreement received*
>
> *Definition 29: Group-related net raw agreement received*
>
> *Definition 30: Group-related net percentage of agreement received*
>
> *Definition 31: Group-related raw batting average*
>
> *Definition 32: Group-related net raw batting average*
>
> *Definition 33: Group-related surplus raw agreement received*
>
> *Definition 34: Group-related surplus percentage of agreement received*
>
> *Definition 35: Group-related surplus net raw agreement received*
>
> *Definition 36: Group-related surplus net raw batting average*

The language grows cumbersome, but the basic distinctions are simple ones. Fortunately it is not necessary at this point to fix each of these definitions firmly in the mind.

"ADJUSTED" POWER MEASURES

Having taken into account the group-related aspect of power, we must still confront one additional ambiguity. The scores reflect initiations and receptions of specified subcategories of interaction, namely agreement, disagreement, and suggestions. In some cases we have controlled for (i.e., divided by) the total volume of an individual's initiations or receptions, distinguishing, for example, between the man who gets many positive reactions and the man who gets a high proportion of positive reactions. But just as the use of raw interaction counts ignores intergroup differences in size, tendencies to agree, and so on, so the use of total volume of interaction as a control neglects intergroup differences in individual participation rates. Thus we may want to consider an individual's group-related scores in the light of his group-related participation rates. For example, we can transform

$$\frac{A_r}{\text{group average } A_r} \text{ into } \frac{A_r/\text{group average } A_r}{P_r/\text{group average } P_r}.$$

In this way we take account of the fact that an individual who receives much interaction is likely also to receive much agreement. The effect of this operation is to reduce the individual's score if he receives a lot of comments, relative to the average for his group. Or it can be thought of as the member's percentage of agreement received (A_r/P_r) augmented by ($\times$) the ratio of group average receptions to group average agreement received (group average P_r/group average A_r). In this sense, these *adjusted* scores are combinations taking cognizance of both the member's absolute power and his power in relation to other members of his group. This operation produces nine variables, which will complete the list of 45, as follows:

Definition 37: Adjusted raw agreement received
Definition 38: Adjusted net raw agreement received
Definition 39: Adjusted net percentage of agreement received
Definition 40: Adjusted raw batting average
Definition 41: Adjusted net raw batting average
Definition 42: Adjusted surplus raw agreement received
Definition 43: Adjusted surplus percentage of agreement received
Definition 44: Adjusted surplus net raw agreement received
Definition 45: Adjusted surplus net raw batting average

We have then, a total of 45 indicators of interpersonal power, each theoretically distinct and empirically quantified. Many more such measures might have been developed if other data were available; for example, if we had information on opinions before the laboratory meetings, we might be able to see who actually changed their opinions during the discussions, and at whose urging. But the complexity at hand is bewildering enough. How can we go about reducing it to meaningful proportions? One way would be to approach the definitions at the theoretical level, eliminating measures on grounds of their probable redundancy, triviality, or complexity. The result would be one or several (fewer than 45) "true" measures judged theoretically significant.

An alternative method, employed here, is empirical. The actual relationships among variables are examined to determine whether they are all measuring the same thing—a kind of global power—or a few things, or each a different thing. Are we tapping the same dimension of power when we measure, say, the rating a member gets from others on his influence and his success in getting agreement for his suggestions? If so, we should find a high correlation between these two scores. Does a person's self-rating on influence or his report of his own behavior in leadership roles reflect the same kind of power as is indicated in his participation rates? If so, these variables should show strong positive relationships to one another empirically. A look at the simple correlations among all possible pairs of the 45 variables shows at once that the first possibility — all measures are tapping a single power dimension — is not borne out. There is a wide range of variation in the strength of relationships, ranging from the .90's to the −.50's. But pair-by-pair analysis, considering relationships between variable *A* and variable *B,* soon becomes more confusing than enlightening. What we need is a multivariate technique, one that will enable us to consider simultaneously dependencies among many variables. For that purpose, factor analysis has proved most useful.

FACTOR ANALYSIS RESULTS: FIVE DIMENSIONS OF POWER

"Factor analysis is a technique which can be used to take a large number of operational indices and reduce them to a smaller number of conceptual variables."[12] A factor is an underlying dimension or component to which the individual variables are related. In other words, factor analysis sorts the variables into clusters according to their relationships to a hypothetical new set of more fundamental and inclusive variables, the factors.

There are a variety of methods for factor analysis which can be used for different purposes. The method used here is a principal component method, by which orthogonal or right-angle factors are sought.[13] That is, the factors are by definition uncorrelated with one another and thus would appear in a graph as lines intersecting at right angles. Thus we are looking for underlying dimensions representing *different, independent* aspects of power. The method used imposes this approach — it seeks orthogonal factors — but the method does not determine positive findings, in that it may turn out that all variables are highly correlated with one factor or with a few or with many.[14]

[12]Hubert Blalock, *Social Statistics* (New York: McGraw-Hill, 1960), p. 383. For a critique of small groups factor-analysis studies, see Golembiewski, pp. 78ff.
[13]For a technical discussion of principal-component factor analysis, see Harry H. Harman, *Modern Factor Analysis* (Chicago: University of Chicago Press, 1960), ch. 9.
[14]It should be noted that factor analysis assumes linear or straight-line relationships among variables.

Before submitting data for factor analysis to the computer, one must make certain fairly arbitrary decisions. Then in presenting the data certain specifications of interpretation must be chosen. But it should be emphasized that these criteria are general ones which do not permit discretion regarding individual variables. For example, one does not excise a variable from a factor pattern because it is difficult to understand why the computer put it in a certain place. The data fed into the machine may be called into question and the interpretation of the results may be uncertain, but the intervening process, once certain preliminary decisions have been made, is ruthless and exact.

I decided to obtain (or extract) ten factors; this was arbitrary — a greater or lesser number might have been selected. The first step in the process produces an unrotated principal component factor pattern, which is derived on the basis of accounting for as much of the variation (variance) in the data as possible with the fewest factors. Here the first factor is the one which explains or accounts for the largest possible amount of variance, the second accounts for less, the third still less, and so forth, up to ten factors. This initial factor solution almost always results in a single dominant factor, clustering many of the variables together and explaining a considerable amount of the variance, and several other, less weighty factors. The big difficulty in interpreting the unrotated pattern is that many individual variables turn out to be significantly correlated with more than one factor. For example, suppose variable X has a factor loading (correlation coefficient between variable and factor) of .666 on the first factor and .555 on the second factor. With which cluster of variables does it belong? In a sense it looks like some of both. When there are many such cases, the interpretation is difficult because the groupings are ambiguous.

To clarify the meaning of these multiple relationships a second step, rotating the factors, can be performed. The rotated pattern arranges the data so as to reveal the simplest or least ambiguous structure. That is, the factors are extracted not in the order of the variance they explain, but in such a way as to maximize the number of very high and very low loadings. Ideally any one variable would load very highly on one and only one factor, and would have zero or near-zero loadings on all other factors. The requirement set for the computer, then, is to approximate this situation as nearly as possible. The factors are still kept uncorrelated with one another, so that they represent independent dimensions, but the variables are clustered in a more readily interpretable fashion.

The ten factors extracted in the present case accounted for 75.4 per cent of the variance in the data. In Table VII.2, the major dimensions of the rotated factor pattern are presented; they consist of the five factors which ranked first through fifth in the amount of variance explained, for a total of 54.4 per cent. Thus the variables which do not appear in the table either showed rather insignificant loadings throughout the pattern or they loaded heavily on some factor which accounts for a rather insignificant proportion of the total variance.[15]

In Table VII.2, then:

1. All variables which load at least .400 (positive or negative) on any one of the five factors are listed.
2. Each variable is listed in order according to the factor on which it loads most heavily — first those variables with the maximum loading on Factor I, then those which load most heavily on Factor II, and so forth.
3. All loadings greater than .500 in magnitude (positive or negative) are boxed. Loadings between .400 and .499 are underlined.
4. In the list of variables to the left of the pattern, I have underlined the most frequent common element. For example, Factor I appears to be dominated by *attributed* power variables.

A brief summary of the elements in the list of IPA variables may be helpful in reading the factor pattern. It will be recalled that:

Per cent means that the basic Agreement and Disagreement scores are expressed as a proportion of everything the member receives. Other scores are expressed in absolute or *raw* terms.

Net means that Disagreements received have been subtracted from Agreements received, in order to focus on the member's net or marginal power.

Batting average means the basic score divided by the number of Suggestions a member makes, e.g., how much Agreement received per Suggestion advanced.

Surplus refers to a "cost" consideration: for a particular member on a particular score, the influence of the other members on him is subtracted from his influence on them, thus showing his excess or surplus of influence.

---

[15]Varimax rotation was used. A positive factor loading means that the variable correlates positively with the factor as defined. Truncation removes from consideration some interesting factors which account for relatively little variance and some variables which do not reach any loading of .400. The following variables had high loadings on other factors: independence in social relations, and dependence as follower; desire to be leader; group-related and adjusted surplus net raw agreement received; adjusted raw agreement received; group-related net raw batting average.

TABLE VII.2

Rotated Factor Pattern, Five Major Factors

Definition No.	Variable	Factors I	II	III	IV	V
8	Average attributed leadership	.967	-.021	.087	.033	.012
2	Attributed influence	.890	-.041	.071	-.063	.038
3	Attributed best ideas	.872	-.089	.174	.072	.019
4	Attributed guidance	.847	-.061	.086	-.058	.141
7	Attributed initiative and ability	.795	.005	.078	.108	.013
6	Attributed likeability	.788	-.010	-.047	.085	-.103
17	Group-related receptions	.681	-.252	.345	-.249	.104
1	Chairmanship	.598	-.124	.006	-.188	.183
5	Attributed friendliness	.566	-.100	.026	.012	-.042
16	Group-related initiations	.539	-.346	.435	.175	.173
27	Surplus net raw batting average	-.518	.268	-.152	.030	.063
40	Adjusted raw batting average	-.044	.918	-.065	.063	.010
45	Adjusted surplus net raw batting average	-.147	.854	-.170	-.051	.039
31	Group-related raw batting average	.059	.789	.223	.333	.031
22	Raw batting average	.003	.777	.230	.237	-.009
23	Net raw batting average	.016	.672	.169	.099	.029
36	Group-related surplus net raw batting average	-.393	.658	-.093	.026	.155
18	Raw agreement received	.459	-.069	.729	.112	.150
26	Surplus net raw agreement received	-.194	.167	.723	.266	.337
20	Net raw agreement received	.416	.053	.700	.315	.086
28	Group-related raw agreement received	.524	-.122	.677	.036	.275
24	Surplus raw agreement received	-.221	-.165	.647	.240	.417
15	Winning proposals	.320	.074	.618	.051	.023
29	Group-related net raw agreement received	.473	.071	.534	.342	.146
21	Net percent agreement received	.005	.213	.159	.882	.106
30	Group-related net percent agreement received	.110	.175	.149	.823	.019
19	Percent agreement received	-.132	.167	.148	.813	.215
25	Surplus percent agreement received	-.107	-.067	.249	.693	.475
39	Adjusted net percent agreement received	.019	.381	-.100	.562	.020
38	Adjusted net raw agreement received	.369	-.322	.313	.465	.207
34	Group-related surplus percent agreement received	.051	-.013	.114	.090	.842
42	Adjusted surplus raw agreement received	.101	.242	.144	.164	.825
33	Group-related surplus raw agreement received	.031	.173	.332	-.238	.803
43	Adjusted surplus percent agreement received	.141	-.244	.062	.116	.787

Group-related means the member's score is taken as a ratio to the average score for members of his group.

Adjusted indicates a group-related score controlled for (divided by) the member's group-related receptions.

INTERPRETING THE MAJOR FACTORS

The computer delivers the factor loadings automatically; naming and interpreting them is a matter of judgment. A method which conforms to common sense is to notice (*a*) the definitional characteristics of the one or two variables which have the highest loadings on a factor—the ones that correlate most strongly with the underlying dimension, and (*b*) the characteristics common to all or most of the variables with high loadings on the factor.

What the factor pattern shows is five distinct dimensions of interpersonal power, each dimension characterized by a clear and theoretically meaningful type of definition. In the paragraphs below the main elements of these five factors are described, using the criteria specified above.

Factor I: Attributed Leadership

A glance at the top variables listed under Factor I reveals the major dimension being tapped. The heaviest loader is Average attributed leadership which is the mean of the individual's scores on the six sociometric items. This has a correlation with, or loading of, .967 with Factor I, and thus accounts for .967 squared, or 94 per cent, of the variance in the factor—the highest loading in our entire collection. It is immediately followed by five of the six attributed leadership variables, with Attributed friendliness trailing shortly behind. Obviously the main distinctive feature of Factor I is its stress on a favorable reputation with the members of one's group. As our earlier examination of correlations among these sociometric items hinted, these loadings give evidence that there is indeed a *generalized,* unitary dimension underlying these ratings on a variety of different criteria. Attributions tend to cluster together, almost regardless of the criteria specified. (One wonders if the same pattern would emerge if a still wider range of characteristics were rated, e.g., energy, appearance, judgment, power in the larger community, and so on.)

The other loadings on Factor I are also interesting. A high reputation tends to be accompanied by a high rate of receptions and, to a lesser degree, of initiations. This reflects the relationship we have already noted between participation rates and sociometric ratings (see above, p. 131). And the chairmanship shows a moderately strong relationship to this cluster. The implication is that centrality in the communications pattern of the group, reinforced by the authority of formal leadership position, is a usual concomitant of respect. Causality probably runs both ways in this relationship: reputation for effectiveness and ability increases one's chances of gaining the attention and confidence of the members, which in turn stimulates one to participate, which increases one's reputation, and so forth. Looking down the list of Factor I loadings on other variables, we notice respectable (although not the highest) loadings for four varieties of agreement received, indicating that attributed leadership also tends to attract a healthy number of expressions of consent and support.

The loading for the last of the Factor I variables is puzzling, however. Surplus net raw batting average shows a moderately *negative* loading, −.518, on Factor I. We might have expected members with high reputed influence to excel on this combination variable, in which one's contributions to the batting averages of other are subtracted from one's own batting average. How is this to be explained? Another way of looking at this loading is that the person who scores *high* on Surplus net raw batting average is unlikely to receive high ratings from his fellow members. The reason for this is unclear, but it may be that a person scoring high on this variable is dominating others, imposing on them, demanding too much of them. They may continue to agree with many of his suggestions on substantive grounds, but at the same time feel a certain resentment which detracts from his popularity.[16] By contrast, the man who scores high on the Factor I variables does not make such extreme demands. While he gathers in a good deal of agreement, he also gives away a good deal of agreement to others, and he makes many more suggestions than he gets direct expressions of consent for.[17]

In any case, our first underlying dimension of power in these groups is clearly the kind which is measured by the most common small groups techniques: attributions, participation rates, and formal leadership role.

---

[16]The simple correlation of "surplus net raw batting average" with "average attributed leadership" is -.48; with "attributed influence," -.51. Notice that this kind of resentment does not appear to attach to either surplus influence or batting-average influence taken separately. Loadings for variables with these dimensions one at a time have no correlation to speak of with Factor I. It appears to be the combined impact of both kinds of influence which detracts from a member's popularity. See E. P. Hollander, "Conformity, Status, and Idiosyncrasy Credit," *Psychological Review*, LXV (1958), 117-27; and Sidney Verba, *Small Groups and Political Behavior* (Princeton, N.J.: Princeton University Press, 1961), ch. 8.

[17]See Collins and Guetzkow, pp. 128-29.

Factor II: Batting Averages

The variables with their heaviest loadings on Factor II all contain a batting average component. Only one such variable falls elsewhere in this pattern, and its loading on Factor II, while small (.268), points in the expected direction. The dimension of interpersonal power tapped by these variables is clearly the *rate* of success a member achieves, in the sense of receiving agreement for a large proportion of his suggestions, the simplest form of the variable being A_r/S_i. Again we should recall that this is a different, independent dimension, showing no consistent relationship with attributed leadership. A look at the loadings on Factor II for the attributional variables shows this pointedly — all are quite near zero.

If we suppose that a suggestion offered in these committees is in some sense like a bill introduced in a legislature, and a single expression of agreement is like a favorable vote cast for that bill, this cluster of variables gets at an aspect of success and effectiveness which is familiar from legislative studies. By extension we might suspect that, in many settings, the man who is most active in producing proposals may receive a good deal of attention and may even have a reputation for success, but, in fact, get favorable action on a relatively small proportion of his initiations.

Other Factor II loadings give us some indication as to how high batting averages are achieved. The moderate negative correlation between group-related initiations and Factor II (−.346) and the near-zero loadings for raw agreement received variables provide a clue: a high batting average is achieved by making few suggestions almost all of which receive favorable responses. A person may maximize his batting average by restricting his suggestions to those which stand a very good chance of gaining agreement.[18]

Factor III: Raw Agreement Received

Factor III is a somewhat less distinctive dimension of power, but it begins with Raw agreement received as its heaviest loader and includes five other variables containing this element — plus Winning proposals. Obviously this factor is dominated by the sheer number of acts of consent a member manages to obtain, considered as a lone quantity, as a margin over disagreement received (net), and as either of these in group-related or surplus terms. Unlike the batting average, percentage, and adjusted measures, these Factor III variables involve

[18]Batting-average influentials may resemble the "persistent momentary problem solvers, picked for brief acts as leaders" described in Hare's summary of research by Cattell and Stice, in Hare, p. 325.

no controls for the member's rates of initiation and reception. Power in this sense means simply the ability to gather a lot of expressions of agreement.

Although by definition the two factors are independent, there are links between Factors I and III through some *variables*. A high volume of agreement received is associated moderately strongly with high initiation and reception rates (the simple correlations are .70 and .60 respectively). Also, Factor I loadings for several of the raw agreement received variables are sizeable, although not the highest. But there is no apparent relationship between the attributed leadership items which dominate Factor I and the collection of Factor III variables, nor does Chairmanship enhance one's chances for gaining many acts of agreement. How are these scattered clues to be interpreted?

Looking back at Factor I again, it is clear that it consists primarily of two substantively different kinds of elements—reputations and activities—which tend to be linked with one another empirically. What Factor III picks up is a somewhat weaker linkage between activity rates and the volume of agreement received. Similarly the odd variable in Factor III, Winning proposals, is strongly linked with that factor (.618) but also has some connection with Factor I (.320). What we can say is that the association between Factor I and Factor III is through interaction rates rather than through reputations. To predict a member's score on Winning proposals—initiating the suggestions the group later adopts as solutions to the problems posed in the experiment—we would want to know how much agreement he receives and the volume of interaction he initiates and receives. Sociometric ratings would not help much in this task.

The emphasis on interaction and the occurrence of Winning proposals in this factor point toward the quality of suggestions advanced as the key to high scoring on these variables. Unlike the batting average scores, success on Factor III does not depend on restricting suggestions to safe ones; many are offered which do not get approval, but *among* those offered are the broad solutions the group eventually adopts—and, it seems probable, a good many other ideas and opinions the group finds valuable.[19]

[19]On differences between decisional leaders and low-risk leaders in the United States Senate, see Donald R. Matthews, "Patterns of Influence in the U.S. Senate, Five Approaches," a paper presented at the 1960 Annual Meeting of the American Political Science Association, Figure 1, p. 11; on attributed versus decisional leadership in American communities, see Robert A. Dahl, "A Critique of the Ruling Elite Model," *American Political Science Review*, LII (1958), 463-69; Nelson W. Polsby, *Community Power and Political Theory* (New Haven: Yale University Press, 1963); and Raymond E. Wolfinger, "Reputation and Reality in the Study of 'Community Power,'" *American Sociological Review*, XXV (1960), 636-44.

Factor IV: Percentage of Agreement Received

The heavy loadings here are for variables in which a member's agreement received score is considered as a proportion of everything he receives. The top three variables — the simplest percentage measures we have — are especially strong ($r^2 = .78, .68$, and $.66$ respectively) in Factor IV. Comparing the loadings these variables have on Factor IV with their Factor III loadings makes it clear that controlling for the total volume of comments a member receives highlights yet another distinct dimension of power.

The interesting aspect of this factor is its divergence from Factor II, the batting average factor. From inspection of the Factor II loadings for group-related initiations and raw agreement received variables, we have surmised that the achievement of a high batting average (e.g., A_r/S_i) depends primarily on restricting one's suggestions to those very likely to elicit a positive response. How might a member attain a high proportion of agreement (e.g., A_r/P_r) without this affecting his batting average?

First, the Factor IV loading for Group-related initiations, .175, indicates no regular tendency for Factor IV high scorers to restrict their output of comments as the high batting average scorers do. Second, loadings of Factor III (agreement received) variables on Factor IV are uneven, but the first one, Raw agreement received, is .112, indicating that the Factor IV high scorer neither excels nor fails consistently, in comparison with other members, to get a respectable absolute amount of agreement. Third, the Factor IV loading of $-.249$ on Group-related receptions indicates that the Factor IV high scorer, like the high batting average scorer, tends to receive a smaller number of comments than do other members of his group.

Patching together these hints, it seems reasonable to conclude that the main difference between Factors II and IV is in the types of initiations involved. To achieve a high batting average (II), one restricts his initiations to those which will stimulate a positive response, while to succeed in terms of the percentage of agreement received (IV), one contributes many remarks which receive *no* direct response, as indicated by the disparity between Factor IV loadings on Group-related initiatives and Group-related receptions. For example, a man might feed out facts to the group in such a way that no response is called for. This hurts his batting average (by increasing the denominator S_i) but perhaps builds a certain amount of credit with the group, so that when he does advance more provocative ideas they are likely to receive favorable treatment.

Factor V: Group-Related Surplus

In the variables loading high on Factor V, the surplus aspect seems dominant. All the high-loading variables share this feature, and the magnitude of the loadings is impressive. Furthermore, we notice that the other surplus items in Factors III and IV have moderately high loadings on Factor V. This surplus calculation, as will be recalled, takes account of the cost of power to a member, discounting his power (in terms of amounts, margins, or ratios of agreement received) by his contributions to others' power (in terms of these forms of agreement given).

However, we also notice that surplus variables with batting average components have near-zero loadings on Factor V. In other words, considerations of cost (as defined) do not have any regular effect on power in the sense of getting consent for a high proportion of one's suggestions. The data offer a possible clue as to why this is so. Whenever we control for rates of initiating suggestions, the distinctiveness of the surplus measures disappears. This is probably mainly due to the fact that there is a strong negative relationship (−.79) between the proportions of suggestions and agreement one sends out. Thus the addition of an element containing agreement initiated to a batting average element does not do much to change relationships among scores. It is clear that one can do quite well in terms of getting a high volume and high proportion of agreement at low cost without this helping much in achieving a high batting average.

The characteristic which distinguishes the surplus measures in Factor V is their group-related aspect. As will be recalled, the adjustment made to produce adjusted scores came after these scores were related to group averages, so that "group-related" is also to be understood wherever "adjusted" occurs. This may indicate that the price charged for power varies considerably from group to group; there may be important differences in norms regarding the amount of agreement one is expected to give out in order to get agreement. It is interesting that this is the only place in the entire array of variables that the group-related aspect makes a clear difference.

Surveying other loadings for Factor V, we notice that there is no clear tendency for the high scorer in surplus terms to excel in Group-related initiations or to gather in a great many acts of agreement. Thus it appears that the way to attain a high score on these surplus variables is to practice conservation in supporting others. By taking in a roughly average amount of agreement, but giving out rather less, one can increase his power as defined here.

A word remains to be said about a collection of variables which do not appear in any of the five major factors, namely the six self-descriptions, *Definitions 9* through *14,* elaborated on pages 132-34 above. These and a few other variables show up on other factors which account for relatively little of the over-all variance or fail to reach any loading of .400. Clearly these self-descriptions represent varieties of power, or perceptions of power, not strongly linked with the major reputational and interactional clusters. These questions are blunt instruments, scored in a simple one-way-or-the-other manner, and pitched at a rather high level of generality. Conceivably other inquiries would produce self-perceptions more clearly related to the main factors, but our conclusion at this point must be that predictions based on members' reports of their own power are unlikely to be borne out in practice.

RESOURCES AND INTERPERSONAL POWER

If these five dimensions of power represent distinct and consistent clusters of variables, why? At least two kinds of explanation seem reasonable: a person may attain a special type of power because he *has* something or because he *does* something, or both. We already have some indication of the behaviors associated with the various dimensions and I shall return shortly to that topic. But first we need to explore the resources associated with each dimension.

The data consist of correlations between the personal characteristics of the members and their scores on the two variables which loaded most heavily on each of the five factors. These top two variables can be thought of as *factor representatives,* since they are the ones most highly correlated with the underlying dimension concerned. Thus we will consider Average attributed leadership and Attributed influence as representing Factor I, and follow the same procedure for each of the other factors.

The resources which may have a determinative influence on power scores fall into three general areas: (*a*) *experience,* including age, years in town, seniority on the board of finance, prior experience in public office, activity in civic and party organizations, and social intercourse (occupational time spent talking, frequency of occupational conferences, and frequency of evening visiting outside the home); (*b*) *status,* measured by a composite index of socioeconomic status combining income, education, occupational status, and self-designated social class; (*c*) *affiliation* — meant to tap positive attitudes toward the board, the other members, and one's performance in the role — consisting of (i) one's self-rating as a member, (ii) a summary rating of the board (respondent's own rating of board performance in general and on the laboratory tasks, as well as perceived ratings by citizens and town officials), and (iii) one's desire to be liked (from Schutz's FIRO-2, the rank given being Very well liked rather than A leader or Prominent in the activities as a group member).

For correlations with the factor representatives, the above variables were first used in both raw and group-related forms. For example, age was considered both as an absolute number of years and as a ratio to the group average. The results of these operations were very similar, with the group-related variables producing slightly higher correlations in most cases. Therefore the raw variables are omitted in Table VII.3. Also omitted are correlation coefficients smaller than .15 — ones we can be fairly sure are utterly insignificant.

A glance at the data in Table VII.3 reveals at once that we have not discovered definite and determinative causes for the various types of power. The largest correlation coefficient is .33, accounting for about 11 per cent of the variance in the dependent variable. Thus knowing a man's seniority or socioeconomic status, while it does provide clues to the bases for his power, does not enable us to make predictions with complete confidence; his prior experience in public office or frequency of social intercourse is even less helpful. Interpretation is risky, but the data suggest the following statements regarding the resources linked to each dimension of power and their possible relevance to the kinds of actions we have associated with each dimension.

Resources for Factor I. Attributed Leadership

In terms of behavior, a reputation for leadership appears to be a result of high interaction rates and of giving out a good deal of support to others. We have already encountered one of the main resources which tends to contribute to reputation: the formal status of chairman. Table VII.3 adds to this picture. Attributed leadership is associated, it appears, with seniority and with a feeling that one is doing a good job as a board of finance member. To a lesser degree (or with lower probability), one's age, desire to take a leading or prominent part (as opposed to being very well liked), and perhaps socioeconomic status also enter into the equation.

These findings lend themselves to the interpretation that the reputed leader acquires his special form of power mainly on the basis of his experience with, attitude toward, and activity on the specialized, substantive work of the board of finance. As we saw in the case of active versus passive chairmen, this *task orientation* — plus a willingness to back up the other members when they make suggestions — can contribute to the respect one receives above and beyond that due to official leadership status. My guess is that attributions of leadership in these particular groups go first to the man who may or may not be especially talented in a general sense, but who knows the business of the board and pushes to get it done.

TABLE VII.3
Correlations between Resource Variables and Factor Representatives

Group-Related Resource Variables	I: Attributed Leadership	II: Batting Averages	III: Raw Agreement Received	IV: Percentage of Agreement Received	V: Group-Related Surplus
Age	.16 .24***	.19* .21*			.16
Years in town	−.15	.16 .26***			
Seniority	.26*** .28***	−.22* −.24**	.27***	−.19*	
Prior public office		.15	.18*		
Socioeconomic status	.19* .15		.33*** .33***	.29*** .32***	.16 .21*
Social intercourse				.16	
Organizational activity				−.18*	−.26***
Rating of one's own performance	.32***		.22*		.27*** .15
Summary rating of board		.25** .26***	−.22*		
Desired to be liked	−.20* −.16	.20*	−.16	−.17	

Statistical significance derived by "Z" statistic:
   ***p < .01
   **p < .02
   *p < .05
(See Hubert Blalock, *Social Statistics* (New York: McGraw-Hill, 1960), pp. 305-7, 456-57.)

Resources for Factor II. Batting Averages

Here the picture we have of behavior associated with high batting averages fits nicely with the correlated resources. As will be recalled, the pattern of loadings gave evidence that a favorable batting average is achieved by restricting suggestions to those one is quite sure will evoke a positive response. This *low-risk orientation* may reflect (*a*) age and long expereince in the town, upon which one can draw for relevant ideas and opinions, (*b*) newcomer status on the board of finance, which engenders caution in offering suggestions, and (*c*) a high opinion of the board and a desire to be liked, which motivate one to seek expressions of approval from the others. Not yet ready to exercise a leadership role, not yet persuaded that he is performing as well as he might, such a person tends to do more listening than talking, confining his comments to safe suggestions very likely to meet with approval.[20]

Resources for Factor III. Raw Agreement Received

We have already seen that this factor is linked to the Attributed leadership factor, via similarities of interaction. The high scorer on Raw agreement received is rather like the reputational leader in contributing and receiving a good many (though fewer) comments, but he does considerably better in terms of initiating the major proposals which the board later adopts. My interpretation was that this variety of power owes much to the inclusion of several especially good suggestions among the many offered, as judged by the other members. Looking at the patterns of resources associated with Factors I and III we see some similarities but also some suggestive differences. Both are related to seniority and to a favorable opinion of one's own performance. But the correlation between Factor III and socioeconomic status is stronger than that with Factor I — in fact these are the highest correlations in the array. And the high scorer on Raw agreement received is more likely to be critical of the board's performance.

To speculate tentatively about these differences: the responsibilities of chairmanship associated with Factor I probably incline one to put forth many guiding, mediating, detail-developing comments which facilitate rather than invent solutions for the group's main problems. Unrestrained by this responsibility, and equipped with equal seniority and superior personal talents (insofar as socioeconomic status reflects

[20]See Robert C. Ziller *et al.*, "The Newcomer in Open and Closed Groups," *Journal of Applied Psychology*, XLV (1961), 55-58.

this), the high scorer on Factor III tends to take a more free-swinging, idea-generating part in the discussions. For want of a better term I would call this a *propositional orientation,* exemplified by the member who is able to bring together several strands of argument into a workable set of proposals for action.

Resources for Factor IV. Percentage of Agreement Received

One may maximize the proportion of agreement he receives, we surmised, by offering mainly comments which do not elicit response, such as purely informational or technical contributions. In payment for this type of service, the member may count among the few remarks he *does* receive a high percentage of supportive ones. The resource correlates for Factor IV can be interpreted consistently with this speculation. The *informational orientation* represented here gains strength from socioeconomic status: the member can draw on his personal skills and knowledge for relevant data. For example, a member with considerable education and experience as a business executive may find it relatively easy to grasp the details of a budget rapidly and point out significant relationships among the items. But this is the only type of resource associated with Factor IV (except, perhaps, some practice in verbal communication). Lacking seniority in this particular group or experience in civic or political organizations more generally, a talented member may choose, in effect, to contribute facts rather than opinions.

Resources for Factor V. Group-Related Surplus

The behavior associated with power when support received is related to support given appears to be a restriction in the latter regard: the member adopts a *conserving orientation,* contributing little to the power of others. The implications of the resource correlations for this factor are not entirely clear. The negative correlation with organizational activity may suggest a certain lack of experience in the give-and-take of decision-making. Combined with a high rating of one's own performance, this may represent some lack of social perceptiveness or perhaps simply a feeling that one deserves to receive support without giving much in return. I suspect that more sensitive attitudinal questions might reveal such a tendency, but without them further speculation is unwarranted.

ELEMENTS OF POWER

What are the broader implications of these findings for the study of interpersonal power? Despite the considerable number of concepts, variables, and relationships we have examined, this chapter is only a beginning in the task of simplifying and systematizing the study of power. The recurrence of certain main themes points, I think, to several major aspects of any power situation, any one of which, if neglected, could give an incomplete image of how power works. Thus for each participant in a process, a thorough power analysis would require the following points.

Motives

What does the participant want from the others in the process? His participation may be motivated by any of a wide variety of needs and desires, ranging from getting his way on matters of policy to much less tangible emotional and intellectual rewards. The researcher may choose to focus on the former and ignore the latter, but in doing so he should treat as an empirical question whether or not the participant is motivated toward policy goals. If he is not, whatever effect he has over policy outcomes demonstrates power only in a very special sense.

Demands

Demands are communicated desires. From all the possible kinds of motives which might be satisfied by participation, the participant selects certain ones to be expressed. These are likely to be the ones he anticipates that others in the process can and will satisfy. The man who organizes his actions around the achievement of a reputation for power may, as we have seen, follow a very different kind of power strategy from that of the man who wants approval. The difference between motives and demands points up the importance of the screening process by which a group defines restrictions on and opportunities for the exercise of power.

Resources

What does the participant have that he could use in attaining power? Resources appropriate for the attainment of one variety of power may be simply irrelevant for gaining other varieties of power.

The relevant resources are likely to vary markedly from situation to situation, so that, for example, the possession of expert knowledge may in some cases outweigh great wealth, or aggressive daring may count for more than a pleasing personality. Without some clues as to the resources a man has and their relevance to the political situation, we cannot get very far in judging the extent and nature of his power.

Contributions

Contributions are expended resources. What does the participant "pay" the other participants in order to attain power? As we saw in the distinction between the popular, supportive task leader and the member who hordes his surplus of agreement, different forms of power may be bought for different volumes of contributions to the power of others. Analyses which neglect the costs of power may prove misleading if they confuse an even exchange with a lopsided victory.

Rewards

In the light of all that has gone before, what does the participant actually get for his participation in the process? Whatever it is he wants, asks for, has, or gives, what, at last, does he receive? Estimating the degree to which a participant actually achieves his goals may be the most difficult task of power analysis, because the process is rarely characterized by any definite division of the goods. Proposals adopted by one group must usually be submitted to another; policies decided upon must be executed; judgments rendered may be appealed. Yet along the way there is a series of partial allocations or rewarding events which can provide a rough index of who wins. Lacking such data, power analysis is lost in a welter of guesses as to what might happen if.

CHAPTER VIII

Some Central Problems and Possibilities

PERHAPS THE MOST striking feature of small groups approaches to the study of politics is the vast variety of techniques and findings available. This is at once a hopeful sign, because it offers so many possibilities for improving our understanding of key processes, and a source of frustration, because selecting the appropriate methods and interpreting results of disparate applications require so many knotty choices. Here I will review briefly some of the central problems and possibilities highlighted in the foregoing chapters, asking the reader to keep in mind, as I do, that these generalizations are based on a severely limited set of data.

We began with methodological considerations. Of the many problems involved in choosing techniques, I think the central one concerns the impact of the experimenter-observer on the persons and processes being observed. The systematic imposition of controlled conditions is necessary to generate comparable findings, but this inevitably introduces disturbances which the researcher must take into account in designing and interpreting the research. In planning the research, he will find that informal field observations and intense empathic efforts help him develop a feeling for the kinds of reactions which the subjects are likely to experience in the laboratory. He can then develop procedures which will compensate as much as possible for these reactions in order to bring out phenomena operative in the "real" decision-making situation. Subsequently various tests can be applied to gauge the degree and character of one's success. A strong focus on familiar problems and materials, some exaggeration of the normal task to overcome inhibitions and preclude casual answers, the posing of "hot" issues in relevant but hypothetical terms—these are a few of the ways to counteract the artificialities inherent in close laboratory observation.

The ultimate test of any method is its success in generating useful findings. What the substantive chapters above have shown are some dimensions of government committee decision-making as exposed in the boards of finance deliberations. Since these may invite further investigation, their main features deserve summarization. We have encountered:

1. Calculation Dimensions. The single most difficult and important problem of which the decision-makers are aware is the need to *reduce uncertainty*. Somehow techniques must be developed for simplifying and ordering an immense amount of information, to render manageable problems of great actual and potential complexity. To repeat: simplifying techniques *must* be developed—that is, the option of taking everything into account is not a live one. Some such techniques are inevitable, but this is not to say that the *particular* techniques committees employ for this purpose are inevitable. In fact, as we have seen, some methods for reducing uncertainty, such as defining boundaries of control and concentrating on large and changed elements in the situation, may be undertaken deliberately, although they may also be based on misleading indicators. Other methods, such as focusing on narrowly immediate physical or numerical details, may be practiced more by inadvertance than design, at the expense of broader considerations. The central need is not to pose grand alternative models for approximation in decision-making, but *to work among the limited varieties of realistically available uncertainty-reducing techniques, to invent and evaluate marginal changes in order to increase rationality.* Among the several suggestions we have explored, temporary concentration of attention on certain basic decisions about methods—such as spending a few meetings on organizing information flows—appears promising.

2. Cultural Dimensions. The ancient idea that we know man as a distinctively political animal because he speaks may be outdated by modern research on animal communication. But it points to a significant element of political power—the meanings men express and invoke in the course of exercising power. We cannot hope to understand power by watching what the actors do unless we also listen carefully to what they say—which does not mean that we are to believe everything we hear. The key problems are *to observe and analyze (a) the particular values and perceptions which the actors themselves link with their decisions, by invoking them in the course of making practical choices, and (b) the degree to which the values and perceptions invoked and expressed are subject to a variety of specific interpretations.* Like all social relationships, power relationships among agencies of government are strongly affected by the participants' culture-bound perceptions and expectations. Politicians, like everyone else, act on the basis of what they have experienced and what they anticipate. In the research reported here, we have seen how certain cultural contexts, actually invoked in the course of decision-making, both set conditions for and permit maneuverability in the exercise of power strategies.

For example, time is a limiting factor, in several senses. There is never enough of it. And the present inherits a past and fixes a future. Nevertheless, strategic timing manipulations are possible because definitions of the length of phases in the decision-making process and the order in which they occur are vague and flexible. Similarly, perceptions and expectations regarding cognitive processes, organizational means, and moral justifications channel effort in the pursuit of power. The study of cultural dimensions as they shape decision-making requires answers to two questions: what frames of reference do the participants actually make use of as they decide specific cases? and, how do they take advantage of *ambiguities* in these frames of reference to protect and enhance their power?

3. Personality Dimensions. The problem of linking words and acts is illuminated by our consideration, in Chapter IV, of one way in which personal needs can distort power perceptions when the latter are posed at a relatively high level of abstraction. We saw how answers to a question on the general structure of power in twelve communities appeared to spring more from the personal desires and self-perceptions of the board of finance members, who are probably quite well informed on the matter, than from objective realities. In fact, *the links between personal propensities and general propositions appear to be stronger than the links between general propositions and specific decisional criteria,* in the discussions of power relations observed for this research. This analysis stands as a warning against assuming what may or may not be true in different circumstances, that adherence to some general proposition either reflects or implies its specific practical influence on decisions.

Our data on personality aspects are limited, but at many points we have encountered potentially fruitful veins of psychological inquiry. Why are some chairmen active and others passive? What personality factors enter into the ability of a group to cooperate effectively on their substantive tasks? How do individual members rationalize their places in various power arrangements within the group?

4. Role Dimensions. The critical difference between position and role in these committees is highlighted in our examination of the chairmanship. There is no ambiguity about the position, but the individual's performance in the role varies markedly from chairman to chairman. What emerges is *a definition of the role, not as a set of fixed specifications for behavior, but as a limited but broad* range *of permissible behaviors. Activity-passivity appears as a major discriminant of role performances.* Active chairmen make relatively full use of the potentialites of the role, while passive chairmen act as if they interpret it much more conservatively. These categories coincide with clusters of personal resources, qualitative styles of role performance, and, to a lesser degree, with responses elicited from the group. The findings suggest that research on roles should focus on the *degree* to which the role (e.g., of the chairman) is defined and the *variations* in role performances among incumbents.

5. *Integration Dimensions.* An initial problem in the study of committee integration is that the term has so many possible meanings and applications. One method for selecting among the many available definitions is to gather data related to a variety of integration concepts and then see which of these are most clearly connected with actual behavior in the committee. Applying this technique in Chapter VI, we saw that measures which could be classed roughly as "satisfaction" and "reward" (the latter in the sense of personally rewarding experiences in the group) had little or no regular relationship to various facets of interaction. For example, members who participated a great deal in their groups were no more likely to be satisfied than members who participated little. An examination of some features of group culture helped to explain these negative findings; it is important to take into account shared expectations, so that we do not think, for example, that a member whose suggestions meet with disagreement is rejected in some more personal way.

The main positive findings on integration consist of relationships among various types of interaction as the group deliberates on its substantive tasks. In other words, for these groups the significant facet of integration is *task integration,* a fitting together of questions, answers, agreement, and disagreement in patterns which tend to facilitate the development of solutions for the group's work problems. I suspect that in many *ad hoc,* temporary, experimental small groups, the affective and self-oriented dimensions of the experience are emphasized, at least in the initial periods of group life. The time dimension, the stage of a committee's development, may be of key significance. *The critical problem of integration may shift over time from a major emphasis on interpersonal affective relations to a major emphasis on developing specialized relations to the group's substantive tasks.*

6. *Interpersonal Power Dimensions.* Like the analysis of integration, power analysis suffers from the researcher's tendency to posit one definition, in which he hopes to capture the essence or primary meaning of power, from among a host of plausible and/or interesting alternative definitions. Chapter VII was designed to illustrate how one empirical method, factor analysis, can be used to reduce a considerable number of power measures to a few basic dimensions. This method demands that the researcher postpone temporarily theoretical interpretation of the many varieties of power until he sees how they relate to one another empirically. As it turns out for the particular committees examined here, five underlying dimensions of interpersonal power, each associated with a certain pattern of resources, explain a good deal of the variation in relationships among the 45 power variables.

These results need testing elsewhere; nevertheless, they suggest *that power is neither a unitary nor a totally fragmented phenomenon, but rather that there are a limited, manageable number of different kinds of power, each of which has a specific relevance to the structuring of important decisions.*

From the interpretive standpoint, the data reported in these chapters could be subjected to many other types of analysis. For example, temporal stages in the development of committee decisions need exploration.[1] Methodologically, more experimentation with different groups, tasks, and situations, and the testing of laboratory-generated hypotheses in the field may be productive. The possibilities are manifold, but perhaps they come down to this: if a particular political system consists of identifiable decision-makers who interact with one another, get them together and see how they work.

[1]See Laura Crowell and Thomas M. Scheidel, "Categories for Analysis of Idea Development in Discussion Groups," *Journal of Social Psychology,* LIV (1961), 155-62; and Arthur M. Cohen, "Changing Small Group Communication Networks," *Administrative Science Quarterly,* VI (1962), 443-62.

APPENDIX A

Bales Interaction Process Analysis Categories[1]

Positive Reactions (Agreement)

1. *Shows solidarity,* raises other's status, gives help, reward.
2. *Shows tension release,* jokes, laughs, shows satisfaction.
3. *Agrees,* shows passive acceptance, understands, concurs, complies.

Attempted Answers

4. *Gives suggestion,* direction, implying autonomy for other.
5. *Gives opinion,* evaluation, analysis, expresses feeling, wish.
6. *Gives orientation,* information, repeats, clarifies, confirms.

Questions

7. *Asks for orientation,* information, repetition, confirmation.
8. *Asks for opinion,* evaluation, analysis, expression of feeling.
9. *Asks for suggestion,* direction, possible ways of action.

Negative Reactions (Disagreement)

10. *Disagrees,* shows passive rejection, formality, withholds help.
11. *Shows tension,* asks for help, withdraws out of field.
12. *Shows antagonism,* deflates other's status, defends or asserts self.

[1]Adapted from Robert F. Bales, *Interaction Process Analysis: A Method for the Study of Small Groups* (Cambridge: Addison-Wesley, 1950), Chart 1, p. 9, with the kind permission of Professor Bales.

APPENDIX B

Board of Education Task

PROBLEM #2: RELATIONS OF BOARD OF EDUCATION

A community very similar to yours in another state is seeking your advice as to the best practicable system for running their educational system.

Three broad proposals have been advanced:

Proposal A: The board of education would be a completely separate unit. Funds for operating the school system would be raised by special school taxes, and expended by the school board in accordance with state law. Approval of appropriations and transfers would be the responsibility of the school board alone.

Proposal B: The board of education would be under the partial control of the local government. Funds for operating the school system would be raised by general taxation, and the total figure of the school operating budget would be determined by a board of finance and the legislative body of the community. But once the funds were appropriated, the school board would be free to transfer funds within its own budget without further approval.

Proposal C: The board of education would be under the direct control of the local government. Funds for operating the school system would be raised by general taxation, and all the specific figures in the school budget would be determined by a board of finance and the legislative body of the community. Transfers of funds within the school budget would have to be authorized by the board of finance.

What proposal would your board advise? You may recommend one of the above systems, amend them, or develop a different proposal of your own.

Please arrive at a group decision in 30 minutes.

APPENDIX C

Questionnaires

QUESTIONNAIRE A – 1962

CONFIDENTIAL – FOR STAFF USE ONLY

Some of these questions may not be entirely clear in their wording, or you may be uncertain as to how to answer them. For this reason, there is space at the end for you to add any comments or explanations concerning your answers. Working fairly rapidly, please answer each question, and then note your additional comments at the end.

1. What is your opinion of the *conclusions* reached on the two problems discussed today?

1st problem (Reducing budget)	*2nd problem (Relations of Board of Education)*
____A perfect conclusion	____A perfect conclusion
____An excellent conclusion	____An excellent conclusion
____A satisfactory conclusion	____A satisfactory conclusion
____A not so good conclusion	____A not so good conclusion
____A poor conclusion	____A poor conclusion
____A very poor conclusion	____A very poor conclusion

2. What is your opinion of the *methods* the Board used to reach conclusions on the two problems discussed today?

   1st problem (Reducing budget)   *2nd problem (Relations of Board of Education)*

   ____Methods were perfect   ____Methods were perfect
   ____Methods were excellent   ____Methods were excellent
   ____Methods were satisfactory   ____Methods were satisfactory
   ____Methods were not so good   ____Methods were not so good
   ____Methods were poor   ____Methods were poor
   ____Methods were very poor   ____Methods were very poor

3. To what extent did the members act in the discussion today as they usually act in board meetings? (Check one)

   ____Exactly the same
   ____Very nearly the same
   ____Somewhat the same
   ____Somewhat differently
   ____Very differently
   ____Completely differently

4. What were some of the differences between today's meeting and your usual meetings, in the ways members acted? _____
   _____

5. What were the reasons for these differences?_____
   _____
   _____

6. How long have you been a member of the Board of Finance?____

7. Have you ever been appointed to any other government office?
   ____Yes ____No

   If yes, what offices?   When appointed?

   _____   _____
   _____   _____
   _____   _____

8. Have you ever been a candidate for election to any other government office?

   ____Yes ____No

If yes, what offices?   When?   Were you elected?

_____   _____   _____

_____   _____   _____

_____   _____   _____

9. Have you been active in civic organizations in your town?

   ____Yes, very active   ____Yes, somewhat active   ____No
   (For how long?_____) (For how long?_____)

10. Here are some reasons people have given for agreeing to become Board of Finance members. Please rank them from 1 (main reason) to 4, to indicate how you rated such reasons AT THE TIME YOU JOINED THE BOARD.

    Number 1 through 4:

    ____I thought it would give me a chance to show my abilities.
    ____I believed I had a duty to serve the community.
    ____I felt I would like the company of Board members.
    ____I was interested in the issues the Board decides.

11. Did you originate action to become a member of the Board of Finance?

    ____Yes ____No

12. How likely is it that you would be willing to serve for two or more future terms on the Board of Finance?

    ____Definitely would
    ____Probably would
    ____Probably would not
    ____Definitely would not

13. How would you rate your own performance so far on the Board of Finance?

    ____Superior
    ____Excellent
    ____Fair
    ____Poor
    ____Very poor

14. Have you given any consideration to seeking election to full-time elective office in the future?

    ____Have given it a good deal of thought
    ____Have given it some thought
    ____Have given it little thought
    ____Have given it no thought

15. Generally, during your experience on the Board, which town official, department, or agency has been *most realistic* in its budget requests, so that you can have confidence that they really need what they ask for?

    _____

16. Generally, during your experience on the Board, which town official, department, or agency has been *least realistic* in its budget requests, so that you lack complete confidence that they really need what they ask for?

    _____

17. In your opinion, how well does the Board do in living up to its purposes?

    ____Perfectly well
    ____Very well
    ____Fairly well
    ____Not so well
    ____Poorly
    ____Very poorly

18. Is your work on the Board of Finance about the most important activity you have ever been engaged in? ____Yes ____No

    Attached to the back of this questionnaire is a list of the members of the Board. Please tear off this list. Notice that each member is assigned a CODE LETTER (*A, B, C,* etc.). In answering the next three questions, please identify the members by CODE LETTER ONLY.

19. Aside from Board meetings, how frequently do you see and talk with each of the other members?

Mr. *A* ____Very often ____Often ____Sometimes ____Rarely or never
Mr. *B* ____Very often ____Often ____Sometimes ____Rarely or never
Mr. *C* ____Very often ____Often ____Sometimes ____Rarely or never
Mr. *D* ____Very often ____Often ____Sometimes ____Rarely or never

Mr. *E* ____Very often ____Often ____Sometimes ____Rarely or never
Mr. *F* ____Very often ____Often ____Sometimes ____Rarely or never
Mr. *G* ____Very often ____Often ____Sometimes ____Rarely or never
Mr. *H* ____Very often ____Often ____Sometimes ____Rarely or never
Mr. *I* ____Very often ____Often ____Sometimes ____Rarely or never
Mr. *J* ____Very often ____Often ____Sometimes ____Rarely or never

20. Boards of Finance often profit from having a variety of viewpoints represented among the members. On your board, what associations outside the Board does each member have which enable him to contribute a special point of view in board meetings? (For example, belonging to certain organizations, coming from a particular part of town, having frequent contact with certain groups, and so forth. Please be as specific as possible.)

Mr. *A* _____
Mr. *B* _____
Mr. *C* _____
Mr. *D* _____
Mr. *E* _____
Mr. *F* _____
Mr. *G* _____
Mr. *H* _____
Mr. *I* _____
Mr. *J* _____

21. Please note the CODE LETTERS for the two members (including yourself when appropriate) who are highest in the qualities mentioned:

Who contributes the best ideas for solving problems?
1st: Mr.____   2nd: Mr.____

Who does the most to guide the discussion and keep it moving effectively?
1st: Mr. ____   2nd: Mr. ____

Who helps the group to keep a friendly, pleasant atmosphere?
1st: Mr. ____   2nd: Mr. ____

Who has the most influence with the other Board members?
1st: Mr. ____   2nd: Mr. ____

Who is liked best personally by you?
1st: Mr. ____   2nd: Mr. ____

Who has most personal initiative and ability?
1st: Mr. ____   2nd: Mr. ____

22. In your opinion, should the chairman of the Board of Finance take a strong hand in running Board meetings, or should he stick to routine presiding over meetings?

____Should take a strong hand ____Should stick to routine presiding

23. Compared with most other Board members, how much influence do you feel you have on Board decisions?

____Much more influence
____Somewhat more influence
____Slightly more influence
____Slightly less influence
____Somewhat less influence
____Much less influence

24. What is your political party preference?

____Democrat
____Republican
____Independent
____Other

25. How strong is your attachment to your political party?

____Very strong
____Strong
____Not so strong
____Not strong at all

26. Have you been active in political party affairs in your town?

____Yes, very active   ____Yes, somewhat active ____No
(For how long?_____)   (For how long?_____)

27. Are you a member of the party town committee? ____Yes ____No

28. How different are the Republicans from the Democrats in the town, in terms of:

Their principles and issue stands?   ____Very different
                                       ____Somewhat different
                                       ____Similar
                                       ____Very similar

Their candidates and party members? ____Very different
                                       ____Somewhat different
                                       ____Similar
                                       ____Very similar

29. Which of the following two statements COMES CLOSER to describing decision-making in town? (Check one answer below.)

A

B

Almost all important community decisions are made by a small group of people. These few leaders usually take the initiative in starting projects; they almost always stop any project they oppose. Members of this group frequently get together informally to discuss their plans. Their influence is dominant over nearly all community affairs, regardless of the subject. They seldom find it necessary to concern themselves much with the opinions of other groups or individuals. In short, the town is pretty much run by a small group of persons with a great deal of influence.

Almost all important community decisions are made by a process of give and take among a large number of groups and individuals. On one issue, one combination of interested people will develop, on another issue, an almost entirely different combination is formed. Many different persons bring up important issues for consideration; there is no one group which can stop nearly every project. Leaders find it necessary to pay close attention to what most people are thinking in the community. In short, the town is pretty much run by constantly changing alliances in which many individuals and groups play significant parts.

_____THE TOWN IS MUCH MORE LIKE A THAN LIKE B

_____THE TOWN IS SOMEWHAT MORE LIKE A THAN LIKE B

_____THE TOWN IS SLIGHTLY MORE LIKE A THAN LIKE B

_____THE TOWN IS SLIGHTLY MORE LIKE B THAN LIKE A

_____THE TOWN IS SOMEWHAT MORE LIKE B THAN LIKE A

_____THE TOWN IS MUCH MORE LIKE B THAN LIKE A

29a. Here are four statements regarding the goals of town government. Please read all four statements and then answer the questions below:

A. The main goal of our town government should be to encourage community growth, especially in commerce and industry. Our community has the potential to develop a more favorable climate for expansion. Positive steps should be taken to create better business opportunities, to attract more people to move to our town, and generally to make this a thriving, progressive community. Party politics should not be allowed to interfere with these goals; clean, efficient government will do most to bring about this kind of progress.

B. The main goal of our town government should be to help create and maintain a pleasant, comfortable, and safe environment for community residents. The interests of the people who have made their homes here should take precedence over other interests. Our people generally think along the same lines — they need the convenience and peacefulness of a neighborly community. We should not break up into political factions or blocs, but rather should work together to make this a pleasanter place to live.

C. The main goal of our town government should be to provide essential services without interfering with the freedom of the individual. We should resist the trend toward more government; we should put more trust in the self-reliance of our citizens. Taxes should definitely be kept as low as possible. Political leaders should stress economy in government rather than new plans and projects.

D. The main goal of our town government should be to make compromises of issues as they arise. The views of different groups should be taken into account, and a workable balance reached. The government represents the people; town officials should make themselves available for any citizens or groups who want to get their wishes heard. Politics should keep in tune with the human needs of the people.

30. Of these four paragraphs, which one would you tend to STRESS MOST as an important set of town goals?

　　___A　　___B　　___C　　___D

31. Of these four paragraphs, which one would most members of the Board STRESS MOST as an important set of town goals?

　　___A　　___B　　___C　　___D

32. Of these four paragraphs, which one would most people in the community tend to STRESS MOST as an important set of town goals?

　　___A　　___B　　___C　　___D

33. Would you say that your membership on the Board is:

____Extremely important to you
____Very important to you
____Somewhat important to you
____Not too important to you
____Not at all important to you

34. Generally, what opinion do most *citizens* hold about the Board of Finance?

____Highly favorable
____Favorable
____Unfavorable
____Highly unfavorable

35. Generally, what opinion do most *town officials* hold about the Board of Finance?

____Highly favorable
____Favorable
____Unfavorable
____Highly unfavorable

36. How important are the opinions of party leaders who do not hold public office in the making of town decisions?

____Very important
____Somewhat important
____Of little importance
____Not at all important

37. In your opinion, has the level of town government expenditures in your town in recent years been —

____Much too high
____Somewhat too high
____About right
____Somewhat too low
____Much too low

38. In your judgment, which of the following statements comes closer to your opinion:

____It is impossible for a town government to work effectively without a good deal of "horse-trading" or vote-swapping.
OR
____Political deals, "horse-trading," and vote-swapping are morally wrong and have no place in town government.

39. About how frequently do you get together in the evening with people outside your family?

____Almost every evening
____Several times a week
____About once a week
____A few times a month
____About once a month
____Several times a year
____About once a year
____Never

40. About how many of your good friends are active in—(Check one for each)

political parties?
____Most of my friends
____Some ____Few ____None

town government?
____Most of my friends
____Some ____Few ____None

community organizations?
____Most of my friends
____Some ____Few ____None

town social affairs?
____Most of my friends
____Some ____Few ____None

41. If you had a son just getting out of school, would you like to see him go into politics as a life work? ____Yes ____No

42. On a scale of political philosophies running from liberal to conservative, are you closer to the liberal side or the conservate side?

____Liberal side
____Conservative side

43. Some people say that most people can be trusted. Others say you can't be too careful in your dealings with people. How do you feel about it?

____Most people can be trusted.
____You can't be too careful in your dealings with people.

44. How hard do you find it to disagree with others, even in your own thinking?

____Very hard
____Fairly hard
____Slightly hard
____Not at all hard

45. Would you say that most people are more inclined to help others, or more inclined to look out for themselves?

____Help others
____Look out for themselves

46. Which of these statements applies to you:

____Others probably consider me too opinionated.
____Others probably consider me too indecisive.
____(Neither statement applies.)

47. What is your main occupation? _____
(If retired, what was your main occupation before you retired?
_____)

48. To what extent do you find your occupation satisfying?

____Completely satisfying to me
____Fairly satisfying to me
____Somewhat satisfying to me
____Somewhat unsatisfying to me
____Fairly unsatisfying to me
____Completely unsatisfying to me

49. In your main occupation (or, if retired, former occupation) how much of your time is devoted to talking with others?

____All
____Most
____Some
____Little
____None

50. About how frequently do you take part in conferences, committee meetings, and the like in your regular occupation?

____Daily   ____Monthly
____Several times a week   ____Several times a year
____Weekly   ____Yearly
____Several times a month   ____Less frequently than yearly

51. How long have you lived in the town you now live in? ____(Years)

52. Ten years from now, how likely is it that you will be in the same town?

____Definitely will
____Probably will

___Probably will not
___Definitely will not

55. What was your father's main occupation? _____

56. Were your parents interested in politics and government?

    ___Very much
    ___Somewhat
    ___Little
    ___Not at all

57. What were your parents' party sentiments?

    Father: ___Republican   Mother: ___Republican
       ___Democrat   ___Democrat
       ___Independent   ___Independent
       ___None   ___None

58. Please circle the last year of formal education you completed:

    Grade school: 1st   2nd   3rd   4th   5th   6th   7th   8th
    High school: 9th   10th   11th   12th
    College: Freshman   Sophomore   Junior   Senior
    Graduate or professional: 1   2   3   4   5   6   7   8   9   10
    Other (Please specify): _____

59. Which of the following comes closest to describing the social class you belong to?

    ___Upper class
    ___Upper middle class
    ___Middle class
    ___Working class
    ___Lower class

60. About how much income (approximately) will you and your immediate family make this year, before taxes? _____

61. Ten years from now, do you expect to be making:

    ___Much more income
    ___More income
    ___About the same income
    ___Less income
    ___Much less income

62. Please note below any additional comments or explanations you

may have about any phase of this questionnaire, the discussions, your work on the Board of Finance, etc.

_____

_____

_____

_____

_____

"FIRO" QUESTIONNAIRE[1]

NAME_____

INSTRUCTIONS

On each of the following pages you will find two long statements about how people act and feel in certain situations. Read each of the two descriptions carefully to see how well it fits you. Then decide which of these two most accurately describes how you feel and act. In some cases neither description may describe how you feel and act; if so, estimate which one *COMES CLOSER* to describing your average behavior. Then at the bottom of the sheet, circle the answer that fits you best.

Please be as FRANK and FORTHRIGHT as you possibly can be. Do not hesitate to use any of the categories if you honestly feel that they are most appropriate. Think each question over carefully.

PLEASE PUT DOWN
HOW YOU ACTUALLY FEEL AND ACT,
NOT HOW YOU OUGHT TO OR WOULD LIKE TO ACT.
THIS IS VERY IMPORTANT.

(F1)

A	B
I try to keep my relations with people on a fairly impersonal basis. I really don't enjoy getting too involved with people, partly	I try to make friends as quickly as possible with virtually everyone I meet. To me, being liked is the most important thing.

[1]William G. Schutz, *FIRO: A Three-Dimensional Theory of Interpersonal Behavior* (New York: Holt, Rinehart and Winston, 1960), pp. 220-24. Reprinted with permission of Dr. Schutz.

because it interferes with my desire to be by myself. I don't especially appreciate people coming to visit me at any hour, though I do recognize they're just trying to be friendly. There are many times I don't feel like seeing people – I'm content with what I'm doing.

I feel that I can handle my personal problems better by myself. If I want to talk about them with anyone I would rather it be someone I don't know well than a close friend. In a group I don't get involved with personalities but prefer to stick to what we're supposed to be doing.

I try to have my relationships with people informal and very close. I like to discuss personal problems with close friends. I like people to drop in on me at almost any hour of the day or night, and practically always I will go out somewhere with them if they ask me to. I will go out of my way to make people like me and do a great deal to avoid being disliked by them. Sharing experiences and being partly responsible to others is very important. In a group I almost always try to get to know the other members well because I enjoy the group more then.

Circle the Answer That Best Describes
the Way You REALLY Act and Feel

I AM MUCH MORE LIKE A THAN I AM LIKE B	I AM SOMEWHAT MORE LIKE A THAN I AM LIKE B	I AM SLIGHTLY MORE LIKE A THAN I AM LIKE B
I AM SLIGHTLY MORE LIKE B THAN I AM LIKE A	I AM SOMEWHAT MORE LIKE B THAN I AM LIKE A	I AM MUCH MORE LIKE B THAN I AM LIKE A

(F2)

C

When I am responsible for organizing and carrying out a task, the most important thing to me is to try to include those who are working with me in the decisions and the responsibility I have. I consult them before I

D

When I am responsible for organizing and carrying out a task, the most important things I try to do are make sure everyone knows exactly what is expected of him and make sure I know my job thoroughly. Then I try to see to it

179

make a decision, and we discuss it and try to come to agreement about what should be done. After the discussion I try to divide up the task and have everyone take responsibility for his own part. Then if anyone fails to do what he should, it's up to him to correct it. When someone does fail to do his job I usually don't exert my authority but let the group work it out themselves.

that the task is carried out according to the rules laid down. If I let anyone violate the rules we're following without being disciplined, I lose the respect of those under me, my authority and effectiveness are endangered, and it is not fair to those who are doing their job. Sometimes it is necessary to make an example of someone by disciplining him publicly so that the others know the rules are being enforced.

Circle the Answer that Best Describes
the Way You REALLY Act and Feel

I AM MUCH MORE LIKE C THAN I AM LIKE D	I AM SOMEWHAT MORE LIKE C THAN I AM LIKE D	I AM SLIGHTLY MORE LIKE C THAN I AM LIKE D
I AM SLIGHTLY MORE LIKE D THAN I AM LIKE C	I AM SOMEWHAT MORE LIKE D THAN I AM LIKE C	I AM MUCH MORE LIKE D THAN I AM LIKE C

(F3)

E

When I am a member of a group with a task to be done, the first thing I try to find out is why I am being asked to do it. I feel I have a right to know just what the purpose of the task is, why I am being asked to do my particular part, and what the basis is for all the instructions that the organizer gives. If I object to doing some part of the job I try to present my arguments to the organizer, even

F

When I am a member of a group with a task to be done, the first thing I try to find out is exactly what is expected of me. I feel I have a right to be told clearly what I am to do and precisely what the rules are under which I am to operate. I then try to carry out my instructions to the best of my ability. If I have any questions I feel I should be able to go the organizer and have if it perhaps delays the task, because I feel no one has the right to ask people to do something without giving reasons for it. It is better for each member to take some responsibility for the overall task, because together they will usually know more about how to do it than the organizer. Besides, this way of carrying out the job insures fair treatment for all and the most efficiency.

my questions cleared up. If I object to some of the things I am to do, I usually do them first, then later tell the organizer my disagreement so he can take account of it. However, it is likely he knows what he is doing or he wouldn't have been put in charge. This way of carrying out the job is fairest for all and most efficient.

Circle the Answer That Best Describes
the Way You REALLY Act and Feel

I AM MUCH MORE LIKE E THAN I AM LIKE F	I AM SOMEWHAT MORE LIKE E THAN I AM LIKE F	I AM SLIGHTLY MORE LIKE E THAN I AM LIKE F
I AM SLIGHTLY MORE LIKE F THAN I AM LIKE E	I AM SOMEWHAT MORE LIKE F THAN I AM LIKE E	I AM MUCH MORE LIKE F THAN I AM LIKE E

(F4)

G

When I am with a group of people I ordinarily don't try to participate very much. I almost always sit back and listen to what the others say much more than I talk. When I do talk it is usually just a sentence or two. I rarely make a very long contribution. Also most of the time I respond to someone else's question rather than initiating anything on my own. Perhaps I don't participate in groups as much as I should.

H

When I am with a group of people I try to take a very prominent part. I almost always try to be in the limelight. I don't like to remain silent very long and almost always try to get into the thick of a discussion before long. Sometimes I even say something startling, partly to get recognized. For whatever reason I am almost always one of the highest participators in any group. Perhaps I even overdo it somewhat.

Circle the Answer that Best Describes
the Way You REALLY Act and Feel

I AM	I AM	I AM
MUCH MORE	SOMEWHAT	SLIGHTLY
LIKE G	MORE LIKE	MORE LIKE
THAN I AM	G THAN I	G THAN I
LIKE H	AM LIKE H	AM LIKE H
I AM	I AM	I AM
SLIGHTLY	SOMEWHAT	MUCH MORE
MORE LIKE	MORE LIKE	LIKE H
H THAN I	H THAN I	THAN I AM
AM LIKE G	AM LIKE G	LIKE G

(F5)

Circle the appropriate answer:

A. When I get into a group I TRY to become a leader:
   Usually   Sometimes   Almost never   Never
B. When I get into a group I BECOME a leader:
   Always   Usually   Sometimes   Almost never
C. When I am a leader I am usually:
   Excellent   Very good   Fair   Not so good

Rank the three possibilities given below by placing a (1) before that most desired; a (2) before that next desired; and, a (3) before that least desired.

D. When I am in a group, the thing I like most is to be:
   _____ a. Very well liked
   _____ b. A leader
   _____ c. Prominent in the activities

"POP" QUESTIONNAIRE[2]

NAME_____

INSTRUCTIONS

On each of the following pages you will find a pair of statements about behavior aspects of home life of children. First, you are to read

[2]Schutz, pp. 227-28. Reprinted with permission of Dr. Schutz.

each single statement carefully to see how it fits you. In some cases the statement may not describe exactly how you feel and act; in these cases, estimate which answer COMES CLOSEST to describing your characteristic behavior. Then, at the bottom of the sheet, circle the answer which fits you best.

Please be as FRANK and as FORTHRIGHT as you possibly can. Do not hesitate to use any of the categories if you honestly feel they are most appropriate. Think each question over carefully. Put down your considered judgment as to HOW YOUR HOME ACTU-ALLY WAS, when you were a child.

(P1)

1	2
When I was a child my parents actually spent relatively little time interacting with me. I didn't have the feeling very often that they were very much interested in what I was interested in. They didn't spend much time just playing with me instead of doing what they wanted to do. As a result, I really didn't get to know my parents very well. That is, I'd never see them in very many situations so that I'd get to know how they act and feel in a large variety of circumstances.	When I was a child my parents centered their attention around me. As soon as they were home they would play with me and talk to me and take a great interest in whatever I was doing. We'd interact under all sorts of conditions so that I'd see my parents laugh and cry and get angry, be delighted, and feel fearful. As a result I got to know them very well so that I feel I understand them thoroughly and everything I do is of great interest to them.

Circle the Answer That Best Describes
the Way You REALLY Act and Feel

MY HOME WAS MUCH MORE LIKE 1 THAN IT WAS LIKE 2	MY HOME WAS SOMEWHAT MORE LIKE 1 THAN IT WAS LIKE 2	MY HOME WAS SLIGHTLY MORE LIKE 1 THAN IT WAS LIKE 2
MY HOME WAS SLIGHTLY MORE LIKE 2 THAN IT WAS LIKE 1	MY HOME WAS SOMEWHAT MORE LIKE 2 THAN IT WAS LIKE 1	MY HOME WAS MUCH MORE LIKE 2 THAN IT WAS LIKE 1

(P2)

3	4
When I was a child my home was one in which there was strict discipline. My parents decided what was best for the children and enforced their decision. If we didn't comply we were punished for it. There was very little effort made to teach me how to do things on my own or to make me independent.	When I was a child there was no guidance in my home. I was always given complete independence to do whatever I wanted. Even at a very young age I was on my own and had to do things for myself. There was hardly ever anyone around to show me how to do things or tell me what was right or what was wrong.

Circle the Answer That Best Describes the Way You REALLY Act and Feel

MY HOME WAS MUCH MORE LIKE 3 THAN IT WAS LIKE 4	MY HOME WAS SOMEWHAT MORE LIKE 3 THAN IT WAS LIKE 4	MY HOME WAS SLIGHTLY MORE LIKE 3 THAN IT WAS LIKE 4
MY HOME WAS SLIGHTLY MORE LIKE 4 THAN IT WAS LIKE 3	MY HOME WAS SOMEWHAT MORE LIKE 4 THAN IT WAS LIKE 3	MY HOME WAS MUCH MORE LIKE 4 THAN IT WAS LIKE 3

(P3)

5	6
When I was a child my home was very reserved and unemotional. My parents rarely expressed affection to me. They really did not believe in displaying emotions. It was more a matter-of-fact businesslike atmosphere. Expressions of affection either simply never arose or else were actively discouraged.	When I was a child there was a great display of love and affection in my home. In their own ways both my parents expressed their love for me very openly and without reservation, so that I always had the feeling I was completely loved for myself alone. There was a great emphasis on expressing affection.

Circle the Answer That Best Describes
the Way You REALLY Act and Feel

MY HOME WAS MUCH MORE LIKE 5 THAN IT WAS LIKE 6	MY HOME WAS SOMEWHAT MORE LIKE 5 THAN IT WAS LIKE 6	MY HOME WAS SLIGHTLY MORE LIKE 5 THAN IT WAS LIKE 6
MY HOME WAS SLIGHTLY MORE LIKE 6 THAN IT WAS LIKE 5	MY HOME WAS SOMEWHAT MORE LIKE 6 THAN IT WAS LIKE 5	MY HOME WAS MUCH MORE LIKE 6 THAN IT WAS LIKE 5

INDEX

PRINTED IN U.S.A.